Reflections From a Business Coach

by Dr. Keith Barton

iUniverse, Inc.
New York Bloomington

Reflections From a Business Coach

Copyright © 2008 by Dr. Keith Barton

All rights reserved. No part of this book may be used or reproduced by any means, graphic, electronic, or mechanical, including photocopying, recording, taping or by any information storage retrieval system without the written permission of the publisher except in the case of brief quotations embodied in critical articles and reviews.

iUniverse books may be ordered through booksellers or by contacting:

iUniverse
1663 Liberty Drive
Bloomington, IN 47403
www.iuniverse.com
1-800-Authors (1-800-288-4677)

Because of the dynamic nature of the Internet, any Web addresses or links contained in this book may have changed since publication and may no longer be valid. The views expressed in this work are solely those of the author and do not necessarily reflect the views of the publisher, and the publisher hereby disclaims any responsibility for them.

ISBN: 978-1-4401-1113-6 (pbk)
ISBN: 978-1-4401-1114-3 (ebk)

Printed in the United States of America

iUniverse rev. date: 12/18/2008

Other Books by Keith Barton

Fiction

High Rise
Camouflage
The Protocol
The Reunion
Symbiosis
Low Country
Night Moves
The Kauai Connection

Non-fiction

Reflections From a Psychologist: An Autobiography
Silly Little Love Poems
Retirement is for Sissies

Dedication

Strengths that I have are diligence, persistence, and a love of learning. My parents stressed a better education to get ahead. They sacrificed so that we might have the best schools, the best teachers, and they instilled a love of learning.

Dr. Robert K. Young was my graduate advisor at UT Austin and was my mentor for my Ph.D. in psychology. He was studious but also knew when to have fun and treated us like colleagues.

Dr. William Hollister was my mentor at UNC Department of Psychiatry at UNC-Chapel Hill; he was an accomplished playwright, musician, and psychiatrist. My next two years were full of learning and teaching in a new service delivery system of community mental health centers in the early 70s. Other mentors would come along: Dr. Charles Chadwell, Dr. Charles Barnett, Dr. John Carley, Dr. Jon Hannum, and others who guided my career in state government. Later I quit state government in 1986 and went into business for myself, running group homes for persons with mental retardation. It was a hectic but rewarding four years that took a toll on my health; I sold the business in 1990 to begin a private practice in Houston, Texas, where I continue to work, doing some business and writing coaching part-time.

Drs. Ben Dean, Anne Durand, and Randi Smith continue to mentor my coaching career and I owe much to them for their keen insight and faith in me. I hope someday to mentor younger coaches to repay the favor.

Introduction

Why would anyone want to coach businessmen and women who may be tired of their corporate careers or may just want to turn their hobby into a business? Why would anyone want to be a coach? I've asked myself these and other questions many times when I left the "safe" world of being a therapist where the rules of engagement are well prescribed. It's safer in being the expert whose job it is to listen and help reassure folks that they are not losers, that there's meaning in their lives, that all they need is to have a passion for life. The world of coaching is a different arena where coach and client are equal and the coach's job is to "ask the right questions" to get his or her clients to engage in a plan of action that hopefully will change their lives. So what are my credentials that allow me to work with executives and small business people who desire to take control of their business and financial well-being? First, one must be a graduate of the many fine coaching programs that are available. I happened to choose MentorCoach, LLC, which is accredited by the International Coach Federation (ICF), the governing body of coaches' ethics and practices. Ben Dean, Ph.D. MCC, is the CEO and an excellent clinician and coach who has trained many coaches during his thirty-year career. Ben and I go back to our days as waiters for the football team at the University of Texas when Darrell K. Royal was the coach and won his first national championship in 1969. Ben is a great friend and "servant leader" who practices what he preaches in training others to take control of their career by asking the tough questions. If you're looking for a training program for a coaching career I highly recommend MentorCoach, LLC. You can visit their website at www.mentorcoach.com. First a little bit about me. Although I have been a psychologist for over thirty years, I have been coaching only nine years, and have had the good fortune to meet wonderful people who want something better for themselves. A brief review of my coaching philosophy and experiences follows:

Professional Background, experience and education demonstrating business acumen and coaching qualifications:

- Associate Certified Coach with ICF, since 2005
- Graduate of MentorCoach, LLC ICF-approved training program, 2005
- Eight years of coaching experience with executives
- ICF exam developer and member of MentorCoach accreditation team for 3 years
- Two business start-ups as CEO and COO; successful merger and buy-sell agreement
- Career coach for Ph.D. executives with NIH in Washington, D.C.
- Five-year strategy plan for medical practice
- Needs assessment for Raleigh, NC mental health services
- Client and employee health and safety program in Texas
- Five year plan for Texas Special Olympics
- Ph.D. in Psychology
- Masters of Public Health in Health Administration
- Group process leader for physician-based practices in Houston, Texas
- 150 coaching hours annually since 2005

Impact of Coaching Services

- Successful career transition from CEO to Board Chairman for International Executive
- Five-year plan for five physicians in group practice to allow for transition of President to take on a leadership role

- Business start-up for bank executive for part-time business and allow time to pass series 6 and 7 exams for financial planning
- Due diligence for partnership agreement for COO and CEO for oil services equipment
- AFLAC training for mid-career commission staff in Houston

Overview of Coaching Process

My coaching style is non-directive, whereby my executive clients discuss their current project assignments and managerial approaches to staff recruitment, development, and retention. I use the following strategies to optimize executive growth by:
- Model executive development based on individual and company core values
- Create a visionary approach to problem-solving
- Establish accountability structures for change
- Encourage risk-taking behaviors that foster competition and growth
- Create new markets for your services and products

Quality of Coaching Process

- Strengths-based model vis a vis Marcus Buckingham
- Positive psychology hardiness model vis a vis Dr. Marty Seligman
- Cognitive-learning styles vis a vis Gregorc Matrix
- Results oriented approach to building high-performance teams
- Group process team approach to capitalize on different learning styles
- Emphasis on executive core values and signature strengths
- Familiarity with dealing with Boards of Directors

- Innovative executive development with regard to company and personal core values and beliefs
- Enhanced self-awareness and love of learning
- Shirt-sleeve coaching that models executive behaviors
- Regular direct report feedback using strength-based models and time management
- On-site and virtual feedback for executives
- Emotional awareness on effects of positive feedback to direct reports
- Effective recruitment and career development of promising executives
- Succession planning and role re-definition for senior executives

What is coaching?

Coaching is creating a co-equal relationship between coach and client to facilitate understanding, new skills, and personal growth that is self-sustaining.

Creating the Coaching Relationship

- Acknowledge you have heard them
- Give positive and specific feedback
- Follow through on what you say you will do
- Create a safe, supportive environment that produces mutual respect with active listening and concern for client

Why co-create the relationship with your client?

- Creates a safe, trusting relationship
- Establishes equality
- Customizes the relationship
- Helps the coach know how to work with the client
- Empowers the client

What is a coaching relationship?

- It is confidential
- It is a partnership
- Works on client's agenda
- Respectful and equal
- Benefits the client

Coaching is NOT:

- Therapy of any kind
- Expert and apprentice advice-giver and advice-receiver (mentor model)

Expectations for the coach:

- Use humor
- Use intuition
- Coach to stretch and take risks

Examples of what coach might say at start of relationship:

- How do you want me to be as your coach?
- What do you need from me most?
- If I were the best-ever coach, what would set me apart from others?
- What do you want from this session?
- How will you know you have accomplished your goals?

Coach Promises:

- Honesty and sincerity
- Champion you and your learning and action
- Stick with your agenda

Purpose of Intake Session With Client

- To learn about the client, discovery
- Get a clear view about their view of the future
- Discuss logistics of coaching
- Provide the client with some tools
- Give them a sense of what a coaching session would look like (The Call Focus form)

Sample questions to ask in discovery:

- What fulfills you? What scares you? What do you want in your job? What drives you? Where are you going with your job? What would you do if you knew you couldn't fail?
- What situations are obstacles to your learning? What is your relationship with success or failure? What is the one thing that you must accomplish in your life? What's missing in your life? Who are your supporters? What do you do when you get upset? Angry? Joyful? What are your top five strengths? What do you believe in?

Design the future:

- What do you want to get out of coaching? In 3 months? One year?
- What are you committed to? What do you have in your daily agenda?

Vision of the Future:

- What is your life mission?
- What is your life purpose?
- Are you working to the best of your ability?
- What are you most concerned about?

- Begin to create an action plan and goal—what is the first step?
- What kinds of actions do you procrastinate on? What gets you moving?
- What situations facilitate learning?
- What gets in the way of accomplishing your goals?
- What would your life look like five years from now with coaching?
- Visualize your life balance? What would you like to change and why?

Logistics of coaching session:

- Call Focus Form
- Policy on missed appointments
- Review meeting times, scheduling, vacation time
- Who calls who?

Key Differences Between a Coach and Consultant:

- A consultant tells and a coach listens
- A consultant provides good answers and a coach asks great questions
- A consultant develops professional trust and a coach develops professional and personal trust
- A consultant controls the agenda and a coach collaborates on the agenda
- A consultant analyzes and a coach synthesizes
- A consultant provides knowledge and a coach evokes knowledge

Fortune 500 companies who use coaches value the following traits:

- They listen with empathy

- They establish trust and preserve integrity
- They are deep generalists with a keen sense of observation
- They are big picture thinkers
- They have an eye for winners
- They have power of conviction
- They have detached commitment

Accountability

- What will you do?
- When will you do it?
- How will I know?

Coaching Techniques *

- **Articulation**: describing what is going on with the client; mirroring
- **Clarifying**: use when client rambles or is vague; provides sharper focus
- **Values**: when client is blocked, core value is an issue
- **Acknowledge**: summation of what client is becoming, not just what was done
- **Intuition**: acknowledges client's energy, tone, mood, what is said or not said
- **Metaphor**: I feel like I'm at the bottom of the Grand Canyon in my job
- **Intruding**: Ask permission to interrupt when client is off track; new agenda item?
- **Asking permission**: Can I tell you a hard truth? Can I tell you want I see?
- **Bottom lining**: Be brief and succinct; have client get to the point.
- **Brainstorming:** Take turns without attachment to outcome.
- **Celebrate**: Bringing attention and acknowledgment to your client's progress.

- **Challenging**: Requesting your client to stretch—e.g. I challenge you to make ten calls today.
- **Championing:** "Come on; you can do it." Counter client's self-doubts.
- **Clearing**: When client gets off-track, allow him to set new agenda item or give him 2-3 minutes to clear before getting back to the agenda item.
- **Dancing in the moment**: Being completely present with your client; Level 3 listening; intuitive.
- **Holding the client's agenda**: Coach let's go of his/her agenda.
- **Intuiting:** Trusting one's inner knowing; "I have a hunch."
- **Structures**: Calendars, email, alarm clocks, post-it notes.
- **Reframing**: Providing your client with another perspective.

Powerful Questions

- They invite introspection
- They lead to greater creativity and insight
- Get client to stop and think about what they really want
- They are respectful and nonjudgmental
- They lead to greater authenticity

What the client feels like with powerful questions?

- They are invited to look at new options and opportunities
- They are encouraged to be introspective
- They are invited to be creative and insightful
- They feel respected and do not feel judged
- They are encouraged to pay attention to their authentic selves

What happens to coaches when they ask powerful questions?

- They don't have to be the expert with all the answers

- They forget their own egos and need to be brilliant
- They are respectful and detached from an answer or result
- They invite the client to be curious and creative
- They are collaborators while the client is the expert
- They are more energized

Coaching Presence

- Flexibility (dance in the moment)
- Intuition (what if?)
- Willingness to take risks (why not?)
- Use of humor (Ever feel like Columbo?)
- Ability to see other perspectives (I see your point)
- Self-management (are you ready?)

Setting Goals Using SMART (specific, measurable, attainable, realistic, timed)

- Client should state each goal as positive statement
- Client should write goals down
- Encourage client to set performance goals that are action-oriented
- Help client to "chunk" goals down

The VIM model for action*

- **Vision**: a multifaceted mental image to inspire your client to take action; provides direction and meaning to client; cannot see on our own; requires a third-party.
- **Intention**: a plan of action to bring about change; involves making a decision.
- **Means**: action steps to accomplish a goal; this is generally where we begin.

Vim is a derivative of the Latin term "vis" meaning direction, strength, force, powerful, energy, or virtue.

Thus, coaching involves putting self aside and concentrating on the motivation of your client. The emphasis is on the relationship developed between coach and client where each participates in a process of change that holds the client's agenda using the expertise and experience of the coach. Whereas mentoring involves mirroring for your client what the skill might look like (intention), coaching offers a vision for your client that empowers and holds your client accountable. Success = accountability for change.

* From *Co-Active Coaching*, by Whitworth, L., Kimsey-House, H., & Sandahl, P., Davies-Black Publishing, Palo Alto, CA, 1998.

Format of this Book

This is not a book on Life Coaching which works with individuals around life balance issues such as work, family, spiritual, personal, and career. There are many excellent life coaches that one can choose from on the www.icf.org website who can ably work with folks who want more balance in their life or who want to achieve a particular goal such as weight loss, finding the right partner, increasing work productivity, or a myriad of other personal goals that would make them more productive as *individuals*.

This book will focus exclusively on career change for those individuals who desire to start their own businesses. For some of you, you are in your fifties and can take an early severance package from your corporate job and wish to "go it alone" in the business world. For others you want to start that part-time job that will allow you extra income such as video photography for weddings and special events. For retirees, you may wish to continue working as a consultant or offering small business your knowledge, skills, and abilities. For therapists who wish to change their practice to one of coaching, this book can offer insight into the business skills necessary to make this career move. If you are already in Corporate America and wish to offer coaching to your senior and middle managers, then this book is for you as well.

The book is divided into four sections:

- Setting up your business
- Cognitive and personality correlates of good leadership and managing others
- Career Change Coaching
- Economic Impact on Jobs and Coaching

Table Of Contents

Dedication vii
Introduction ix
Format of this Book xxi

Section One: Setting Up Your Business 1

    Internal Coaches 3
    Negative Coaching Outcomes 7
    Today You Are Your Own Boss 11
    Working for Small Businesses 15
    Office 101 17
    Incorporating Your Business 19
    Branding 21
    Due Diligence 23
    Strategic Planning 27
    Running Your Small Business 31
    Marketing New Clients 35
    Tolerating Instability and Uncertainty 39
    Working Towards Resolution vs. Fragmentation 43
    Practical Ways of Managing Trust 47
    Accepting the Pace of Change 51
    Managing Middlescence 55
    Employee Turnover 57
    Managing Your Business in a Downturn 61
    Net Promoter Score (NPS) 65

Section Two: Personality and Cognitive Learning Styles 69

    The Alpha Male 71
    The Destructive Power of Overachievers 75
    Coaching Entrepreneurs 77
    Coaching Entrepreneurs: Perceiving the Need for Change 81
    Coaching Entrepreneurs: Moving Towards Planning and
        Commitment 85
    Reintroducing Entrepreneurialism 89

Personality or Cognitive Learning Style? 93
Gregorc Learning Styles...97
Emotional Competence 101
CMO: What is It? 105
Crazy Bosses 109

Section Three: Career Coaching.............................. 113

Where Are You Headed? The Career Change Coach............115
Signature Strengths 119
Go Put Your Strengths To Work 121
Core Values 125
Emotional Competence 129
Still Searching for Dream Job 133
Looking For Another Job?..137
Still Looking? 139
Retire Rich?...143
Who You Gonna' Call?..147
Where Have All The Boomers Gone?..........................151

Section Four: Economic Impact on Jobs and Coaching.. 153

Behavioral Economics...155
What's With The Economy?...159
The Financial Markets..163
From Industrial to Cultural Revolution.......................167
The Luxury Generation 171
Energy Consumption..175
Small Business: 100 Fastest Growing Companies.................177
Giving in the 21st Century 179
Wiring the Medical World..183
Target's Secret 187
A Review: *Winning*, by Jack Welch 189
Book Review: *Blink* 193
Peter Drucker: In Remembrance (1909 to 2005) 197
Final Thoughts..201

Section One: Setting Up Your Business

Section One deals with setting up a business that is more than getting a DBA (Doing Business As) at your local courthouse. This book is not about earning extra income with your hobby nor is it about passive income derived from EBay sales. If one is serious about coaching people who want to be businessmen and women then a firm foundation in business law is necessary. The material in this first section will teach you how to: coach business people, guard against negative coaching outcomes, becoming your own boss, working as a small business, setting up your office, incorporating your business, branding, due diligence, strategic planning, running your small business, marketing new clients, tolerating instability and uncertainty, working towards resolution vs. fragmentation, practical ways of managing trust, accepting the pace of change, managing middlescence, employee turnover, managing your business in a downturn, and net promoter scores.

Internal Coaches

Business coaching is different from life coaching because the emphasis is on employee buy-in and performance within the organization. Life balance issues which are critical to personal success at home and work are less important in a business setting because coaching is typically generated from upper management. Therefore, the employee is not necessarily open to coaching at first and the coach must be seen as a facilitator and advocate for the employees rather than management. Unless upper management has bought into coaching for their managers, then any real change is highly improbable.

Recently I was asked to help insurance executives at a large multi-national company infuse coaching into their middle managers. Direct employee reporting had been relegated to "howdy" calls in the field and being available for crisis management. An astute executive wanted his middle managers to become better coaches to their respective field office staff including claims, clerical, fiduciary, and legal personnel. In preparing for the half-day workshop I decided to go back to a seminal chapter in *Executive Coaching* by Fitzgerald and Berger, 2002 on "Coaching from the Inside," by Casey Strumph.

By strengthening internal coaching any gains are more aptly to be accepted because of cultural buy-in. For those organizations resistant to "experts" who typically leave after a presentation with a "bag of tools," a coaching "facilitator" whose job is to teach key organizational players how to better coach may be the answer. Flatter organizations are better suited to internal coaches because of multiple functions and roles where decisions can be implemented more quickly. Certain prerequisites are required, however—i.e.

- A strong and credible HR function

- Executive level support and buy-in
- Using feedback effectively
- Supportive self-development
- Partnering with external experts
- Creating internal coaching networks
- Role modeling and mentoring
- An explicit confidentiality policy

A strong HR department can make or break internal coaching. If coaching is part of one's job description that is rewarded by the company, then supervisors may view knowledge transfer as positive and necessary for successive planning.

Another axiom for successful internal coaching is the level of the employee in the organization. The more senior the executive, the more likely external coaching is needed; in this assignment, I was asked to train middle managers who were critical to the information flow between senior and field personnel. A cost-effective approach was to build coaching into existing job functions, thereby making coaching *part of the corporate culture*.

Witherspoon and White (1998) identified four coaching areas: skills, performance, development, and leadership agenda. Skills coaching can be provided by internal coaches. Sample areas include: conducting meetings, goal setting, and accountability structures. Performance coaching concentrates on improving job performance with growth plans intended to focus on employee strengths and coaching needed to improve skill sets. Development coaching is generally intended for candidates who have just been promoted. Finally, leadership coaching focuses on strategic vision and planning.

Feedback is useful for managers to see if they are actively communicating and supporting their staff; feedback is better given in anonymous surveys rather than 360 evaluations to minimize political agendas. It is important that managers act on feedback given by their staff or give reasons why they cannot act.

Self development includes readings, conferences, structured coaching experience and workshops. Reflection is a valuable tool to improve accountability and provide a timeline for employee change.

Partnering with external coaches is valuable for introducing a new evaluation technique or setting the stage for developing internal coaches within the organization. External coaches can provide validation for coaching performance.

Role modeling is another important function of internal coaches who manage by example and provide an *in vivo* coaching experience for one's direct reports.

Coaching networks are important. The International Coach Federation has state and city chapters that provide ongoing training and sharing of coaching tools and experience.

Internal coaches should secure from management an internal policy protecting coachee confidential information and to share only employee strengths. Trust is gained over time and the coaching agreement should spell out potential pitfalls of breaking confidentiality. The internal coach must face his/her peers everyday and harmonious working conditions require confidentiality.

Helpful Hints:

1. Hire an external coach to give a workshop on coaching within the organization and to validate the importance of internal coaches.
2. Think of a time when you gave negative feedback to an employee and whether or not long-term gains and morale were maintained. Could internal coaching provide a better solution than growth plans?
3. Ask HR if they value coaching and to what extent employee morale and teamwork is improved.

Witherspoon, R., and R.P. White. (1998) Four essential ways that coaching can help executives. Greensboro, N.C.: Center for Creative Leadership.

Negative Coaching Outcomes

According to Richard Kilburg in his chapter "Failure and Negative Outcomes," in *Executive Coaching* by Catherine Fitzgerald and Jennifer Berger, Davis Black Publishing, 2002, coaches do not like to discuss their mistakes with executive clients for a number of reasons. In the client these can be due to:
- Serious psychological problems
- Serious interpersonal problems
- Lack of motivation
- Unrealistic expectations of the coach or the coaching process
- Lack of follow-through on homework or intervention suggestions

In the coach, factors impacting negative outcomes can be due to:
- Insufficient empathy for the client
- Lack of expertise or interest in the client's problems or issues
- Underestimation of the severity of the client's problems
- Overreaction to the client
- Unresolved disagreements with the client about coaching
- Poor technique

Let's take these one by one to see how quickly a coaching intervention can be mired without intent or ineptitude.

Serious psychological problems: Coaching is NOT appropriate for clients who are in need of therapy. One of the first tenets of coaching is not to do therapy which is indicated before any coaching can take place. Remember, coaching proposes an equal relationship between client and coach, unlike therapy, where the client is seeking treatment for a cognitive or emotional block to success on the job.

The coach should immediately ask the client to seek therapy before continuing with coaching and ask the client to sign a release of information for the coach and therapist to share information about the client's progress. The coach can also defer coaching until a certain level of client insight is gained via therapy.

Serious interpersonal problems: Some clients, although not clinically impaired may present unique personality differences that render them unable to accept coaching suggestions. An extreme example would be the narcissistic boss who tries to impress the coach with his/her knowledge and try to use the coach to advance their own agenda with their staff. When confronted with this situation, the coach should respectfully ask the client to seek psychological help before proceeding with the coaching relationship. Some executives can be mean, distrustful, vindictive, and argumentative with their staff and this behavior transfers (bleeds over) into the coaching relationship. The astute coach will quickly recognize that the coaching relationship is unequal in favor of the client and should quickly terminate the relationship.

Lack of motivation: Some coaches are asked by superiors to coach a subordinate who is not producing or measuring up in their job. This is really an HR function and should be handled internally by the company. Unless there is a confidentiality agreement with the underachieving employee, the coach will be perceived as an agent of management and trust will be difficult to achieve with the underperforming employee. Assuming skills sets are present, the lack of motivation could be due to a clinical depression, inappropriate job match, life cycle issue, or interpersonal (e.g. shyness, introversion) characteristic.

Unrealistic expectations of the coaching process. For some clients, coaching is viewed as a therapeutic or mentoring relationship where the client seeks answers from the coach without much introspection or ownership in the coaching process. These clients see the coach as a consultant with "off the shelf" answers to their particular problem in the work place. When the coach is unable to provide the answers, the coaching client quickly loses interest and terminates the relationship.

Lack of follow-through on homework: Unlike therapy, coaching is an active process whereby the client is given specific homework between sessions. Client accountability is key to client success because the coaching client is empowered to assume responsibility for permanent change. When the call focus forms begin to look the same between sessions the client is mired down or stuck, and a rupture in the coaching relationship is imminent and the client will terminate the coaching prematurely to avoid taking on any responsibility for change.

Helpful Hints:

1. Coaches, pick your worst client and see if any of the above negative client factors account for the lack of progress in achieving more positive client outcomes.
2. Clients, ask yourselves if you really want to be coached. Were you asked to enter coaching by your boss, HR, or other third party?
3. For those clients who are in therapy *and* coaching, what do you perceive as the main difference in both relationships?

Today You Are Your Own Boss

The following is an abbreviated chapter from my latest book, *Retirement Is For Sissies,* * which can be purchased on my website (pardon the self-promotion).

In coaching I tell folks who are contemplating starting their own business to devote all their time to writing and sticking to a strategic plan. Retirement is no different. Starting a business after sixty is simple: have fun, work for yourself, stay away from franchises, don't get into family businesses, and work from home no more than two days a week.

Rule No 1: Have Fun

You've been on the corporate ladder for forty years and now it's time to kick back and enjoy yourself. The important thing to remember is to have fun and not get bogged down in details of running a business; if you do, you'll never follow your dream, whether it's a B&B, massaging your stock portfolio, buying and selling on EBay, or pursuing a life-long hobby of photography or travel guide.

Rule No. 2: Work For Yourself

There's an old saying that self-employed either can't work or won't work for anyone else. Working for yourself can be a liberating experience—no more boss, no commute, no meetings, set your own hours and pace, and enjoy yourself. The first step is to decide to pay yourself a salary or 1099 distribution. My preference is to go 1099 since you're only working about 15 hours a week. The next step is to schedule two days a week and spend the remainder of your time volunteering, mentoring, taking courses, and spending time with family. The third step is to network with clients who will buy your service or product. Good resources are trade associations, other retirees, or Craig's list. Finally, devote study time to learn your business.

Rule No 3: Stay Away From Franchises

Fortune 500 had an article this year on why to stay away from franchises. With franchising you work for yourself which defeats Rule No. 1: having fun. Also stay away from other business ventures where you are a silent or passive partner. There's no fun watching your investment tank without control over the business.

Rule No. 4: Don't Work With Family

The only exception to this rule is working with your spouse, assuming you both want to work together and can agree on what you want to do. With extended family, boundaries become diffuse, job descriptions are non-existent or poorly defined, pay is unequal, and succession planning is lacking. You can't be family and employee at the same time with tempers flaring and drama in the office.

Rule No. 5: Work From Home

This is a no-brainer. Why pay for an office when you can work from home? Be sure to keep a separate office and keep track of your expenses. Home office deductions are red flags for the IRS. My wife and I keep separate offices at home with separate laptops, but we share a fax and printer. I suggest you and your wife pick the same two days to work so you can spend more time together.

Rule No. 6: Two is the Number

If you're working more than two days a week, then you're defeating the purpose of your retirement. If you find yourself turning down invitations from family and friends or putting off vacations then you haven't retired. You've just left your cubicle of forty years and substituted a new cubicle at home.

I hope I've given you some thoughts for working during your retirement if you choose to do so. Remember that any money derived from your work is secondary to staying active and learning new things. For those of you eager to embark on new paths during your retirement, the excitement of learning a new vocation without much financial risk can only occur if you're not bogged down with a career. Retirement offers an excellent opportunity to explore new knowledge, skills, and abilities.

Helpful Hints:

1. Start a hobby or avocation now and parlay it into a fun job when you're ready to retire. Make a list of things you like to do for fun and see if there's any work potential.
2. Contact your local SCORE (senior corps of retired executives) for any business opportunities where you might partner with another person.
3. Talk to other retirees who have bought into franchises and ask them how much time it takes and (if they're honest) their return on investment (ROI).

* Retirement is for Sissies: Or how I learned to survive my job. Iuniverse.com press, Lincoln, NE 68512, 2007.

Working for Small Businesses

For those of us who want out of corporate America but lack the entrepreneurial drive and spirit, a small business may be the place to look for your next job. Small businesses have always been responsible for employment rate increases due to the fact that they are run more efficiently through outsourcing and recruit locally. A review of Fortune Small Business fastest growing companies for 2004 include: health care (25%), industrial (25%), technology (16%), restaurant and food services (6%), medical administration (5%), gaming (4%), consulting (3%), oil and gas (3%), building supplies (3%), and other (16%). For the second consecutive year a health fitness company landed the number one position with an 84% ROI. This company helps more than one million patients manage chronic diseases such as diabetes, asthma, and heart disease. As the baby boomers age and live longer we will be faced with a chronic illness in our lifetimes and the medical technology and tools are expanding to help us maintain and treat chronic illness in our homes rather than clinics and hospitals.

Second on the list is a software company that manages data for 150 life science, pharmaceutical and biotech companies around the world. Hospitals, clinics, and outpatient offices will eventually share the same data base, and patient charts including imaging data will be readily available as the patient moves seamlessly from outpatient to inpatient, rehab, and other levels of care during episodic flare-ups with their chronic illness. Arthritic pain, orthopedic advances in joint replacements, chronic fatigue, and other nervous conditions account for increasing employee lost time at work, not to mention cost for prescription drugs.

What this means to those of us who want off the corporate track is to look within our local communities to minimize commute time, parking fees, organizational dues, and endless meetings and overnight travel. Job satisfaction, especially for women, allows greater flexibility in work hours to attend to personal and family matters. Family-owned businesses can be a logical solution to balance professional and personal goals more effectively. In coaching busy executives the number one complaint is lost family time and not placing a higher priority on fun and play. While you might be paid less with a smaller company, one needs to look at reduced business expenses mentioned above associated with larger corporations. Health benefits are competitively priced to allow companies with 100 or fewer employees to compete with the "big guns."

Another advantage to working with a smaller company is to align your core values with those of the company. Those of us who still value integrity, fairness, equality, and loyalty are more likely to see those values reflected in smaller companies. Organizational charts are more flat, pay scales are more equitable and based on performance rather than longevity and small-business owners are more likely to treat their employees as their number one resource for success. Besides a salary, you might find yourself working from home three days a week, using your cell phone from work for personal business, and Friday "ice cream socials." Collegial support replaces competition; casual replaces formal; style replaces branding; and shared profits replace dividends to outside shareholders.

Helpful Hints:

1. Get a copy of Fortune Small Business 100 and peruse the latest issue at your local library. See what small companies are doing for employees besides salary and benefits.
2. Talk to a small business owner and see what s(he) offers to his(her) employees in the way of compensation to boost productivity.
3. Attend a small business meeting with your local chamber of commerce and begin to network with owners. Often, free business seminars are offered on a variety of subjects: perks, performance incentives, employee-shared risk taking, support for innovation, mobility options.

Office 101

Setting up your practice or small business can be a daunting task, but it doesn't have to be. There are many books on the market, but my favorite is "Small Business Kit for Dummies," by Richard Harroch, IDG Books, 1998, that any Barnes and Noble would have in its self-help section. The book is divided into sections covering: starting your business, money matters, employee and consultant issues, bulletproofing your business, spreading the word, web sites for B2B marketing, plus frequently used employee and bookkeeping forms on a CD-ROM. When I set up my psychology practice five years ago, I used this book to help me with my policy and procedure manual, expense reports, income statements, IRS and state unemployment and franchise taxes.

One of the first decisions to make is locating your office. As in any real estate venture, location is primary. You want to be on a bus route and wheelchair accessible. Make sure your building meets ADA guidelines for bathrooms and elevators. I prefer the first floor for accessibility and picked a 1600 square foot office with nice floor to ceiling windows for a greenbelt view while offering privacy to my clients. I share the space and office expenses with two colleagues. Make sure you have a buy-out agreement in your lease if one of the tenants leaves prior to the lease expiration or the ability to sublet the space. Other issues to consider if you're in private practice is to consider the records retention policies and storing your overflow records off-site (either your home or public storage). I've heard horror stories of first floor storage spaces becoming flooded (especially in Houston where I live) and records lost or permanently damaged.

When negotiating your lease be aware of automatic expense increases for maintenance and make sure they are prorated based on your office space percentage of the total building. Also be sure to get liability and content insurance for fire or theft. Three to five-year leases are standard. A+ buildings are preferred to give your business a professional presence. First impressions are important. I purposely turned down a better deal for office space that was located on the second floor above a night club. Even though I had not planned late evening appointments, I didn't want to be known as the psychologist with the office "above the night club."

Now that you have your lease in place, it's time to furnish your office. You want a comfortable, but not too stuffy waiting room. We decided on décor that might fit a living room to give one the sense of visiting a friend rather than a doctor or consultant. Stay away from opaque glass, oversized furniture, hardwood floors, bright lighting, and expensive accessories. You want your clients to be relaxed. We schedule our clients an hour apart to avoid crowding and greet them personally at the door and then bring them back to our offices. We offer bottled water or coffee and they can bring their own food or drink with them if the meeting is during the noon hour. I bring my own lunch to allow more time for my clients. My office is set up similar to my home office and a DSL line allows internet access for research and email.

Helpful Hints:

1. Call around and get a list of A+ building comparisons (comps) on an annual square footage basis. Most run between $10-$15 per year. Our current three-year lease is $12 per square foot per year or $1 a month.
2. Compare office furniture prices at discount stores. Office Max and Office Depot have some great buys, but stay away from particle board. Look at accessories for your waiting area.
3. Fire, theft, and content insurance policies typically run around $500 a year. Shop around for the best prices and look at your lease to see what they cover so as not to pay for duplicate coverage.

Incorporating Your Business

The advantage of incorporating your business as opposed to a DBA (Doing Business As) is that incorporation affords you legal protection of your personal assets. With a DBA, a dissatisfied customer can sue you and attach your personal assets. In the state of Texas, one legal residence (homestead exemption), one car and $30k of furniture and machinery are free from attachment, but you should consult a business attorney or your CPA before deciding on DBA versus incorporation. When the risk of litigation is small and business assets are under 150k, then a DBA may be the way to go. For only $11, one can do a DBA in Harris County, Houston, Texas which is good for 10 years. Contrast this with incorporating with the Secretary of State's Office for about $300. In Texas, one does not pay a franchise tax for annual gross revenues under 150k, but any monies in excess of that amount are taxed around 4%--something to consider for more profitable businesses. Furthermore, by incorporating, you are giving notice to the Feds and state officials that you are liable for monthly tax payments if you pay yourself a salary or have employees. Most solo business owners choose to treat themselves as an employee and gain the advantage of social security contributions in addition to a forced federal withholding contribution. In addition I choose to make quarterly tax payments on my net profits to minimize owing Uncle Sam a truckload of money on April 15th. Most attorneys will do an incorporation for $750 which includes the filing fee with the Secretary of State's Office and getting you a tax ID number from the Feds. Incorporations legitimize your business and are a marketing tool to show the world that "I am really in business." Many home businesses will do just fine with a DBA, but if you're marketing over the Internet doing B2B Commerce, incorporation is preferred.

Dr. Keith Barton

Now that you've decided to incorporate there are many options: limited partnership, Chapter C, subchapter S, and sole proprietorship. If you are the only employee you can choose from any of the above, but most choose subchapter S, because this affords you the legal protection of a chapter C corporation without the burdensome paperwork and filing requirements. Furthermore, you can use a schedule C and file your business income as part of your personal return. Although the deadline for business filings is March 15th, any net income (profit) derived from the business is reported on your personal return due on April 15th. There are advantages to filing as a Chapter C if you have other employees and wish to give employee benefits, including retirement accounts. 401(k) to yourself and your staff. These will be discussed in a later newsletter, but a subchapter S corporation still allows for a Simplified Employee Plan (SEP/IRA) allowing you to save up to 13.1% of your salaried income each year and you are not obligated to contribute the same amount each year. Thus your contributions can range from nothing to the maximum percentage depending on your profitability that year.

Helpful Hints:

1. Before deciding on incorporating your business, talk to your CPA or tax attorney.
2. Talk to others in your line of work to see how they structured their business.
3. If you have a signature mark (sm) or trademark™; check with an attorney who specializes in intellectual property right law.

Branding

This month I want to talk about "branding." When you think about Charmin, do you see Mr. Whipple squeezing the tissue paper? Or how about "Just Do It" launched by Nike. What do you want people to think of when you advertise your business on the web? I decided on a "handshake" logo for the Virtual Executive Coach to conjure the image of sealing a contract or to indicate agreement between two parties. Companies spend millions putting out their name out there to beat the competition. "It's a Chevy" means "heavy duty" or "Ford Trucks are Tough." Now the low carb craze is being pasted on every fast food menu in America today to attract new "dieters" and to keep their current customers from leaving. Branding is all about name recognition. Remember the movie, "Ghostbusters" and "Who'll ya gonna call?" The movie spoof is an excellent example of branding. We have a furniture salesman in the Houston area who pulls out dollar bills from his back pocket and says "Save you money." He has made a fortune and everyone knows "Mattress Mac" whose claim to fame is "buy it today and deliver it tonight; no more back order slips."

Let's talk about niches. Think about what you offer your customers that is unique from anyone else. Why would people want to come to you before anyone else? Is it because you're the most competent, the most charming, and the most engaging? I don't think so. You want to SELL YOURSELF FIRST. In order to make this happen, you need to be enthusiastic about your product or your service. Your website, e-newsletters, letterhead, business cards should each reflect your credibility and position in the industry. Everyone wants to receive services from the best, so make yourself the best you can be (to paraphrase from the U.S. Army Recruiting Office).

Some things you can do to make yourself more visible are to brand your image. To do this you have to strive for three factors according to Dr. Steve Barnett with Global Business Network: 1) your brand should represent you as your authentic self; 2) your product or service should delight your customers; and 3) define your unique skills. Branding can be reactive or proactive. The Accenture brand was an attempt to resurrect the defunct Arthur Anderson consulting group, tainted by the Enron scandal; this was proactive to develop a new image for a once tarnished company. Conversely, adding "low carb" to fast food menus is reactive in the sense that it may protect from potential litigation if someone dies from obesity from eating McDonald's hamburgers (don't laugh, a lawsuit was filed).

So think about your business. What can you do to distinguish yourself in a positive way from the competition, truly represent you authentically, and define your skills? We have many executive coaches, so how would your logo or brand drive folks to your website or get them to email you? I wish I could say my website does this with the "vision plus accountability equals success," but this is pretty generic and how many handshakes does one see in business meetings? Although the look might be formal and polished, it is trite, now that I think about it and there is nothing on my webpage to "whet the consumer's appetite" for more knowledge. On my next major web redesign I will pay more attention to branding as you should.

Helpful Hints:

1. Think about what uniquely defines your company; experiment with logos and symbols that reflect originality, delight, and your services.
2. Go through various magazine ads and see which ones you attend to. What is it about the ad that compels you to want to learn more?
3. If you were a consultant to your own company, what changes would you make to your existing logo or signature lines that uniquely capture the essence of your services or products?

Due Diligence

I have a current client who is thinking about going into business with a vendor of his previous oil and gas equipment company (no non-compete agreement exists). While friends with his prospective partner, this 60-year old former CEO asked to talk to me about sizing up his offer (the names and business sector have been changed for this article). After massaging the numbers and before filing any incorporation papers, company charter, and by-laws (including stock options and voting rights), my client's questions addressed three main issues:
1. Can I trust this guy?
2. Who will control the business?
3. What happens if one or both of the partners become incapacitated or deceased?

After the attorneys, accountants, and bankers do their review of assets, liabilities, inventory, customer lists, and performance trends over the past ten years, the numbers told my client he should make the move and join his friend in this new, potentially highly profitable venture. But he came to see me because of the three nagging questions that I think everyone asks after the numbers are crunched and the money is secured. Let's take the questions in order.

Can I trust this guy?

This goes to the heart of doing business with a partner. The adage was that friends should not do business together. Despite the allure of similar goals and comfort level, my client was angry and confused that his partner refused to talk specifics—e.g. buy-sell agreements, key-person insurance, survivor issues in the event of disability or death, voting rights vis a vis the future direction of the company. My client was offered 49% of the stock (a minority position) which he was unhappy with because while his partner had the inventory and engineering know-how, my partner had the contacts (read contracts) through his extensive networking and 20-year reputation with customers. This translates into a concept called "good will" which lends a certain monetary value to any operation. However, his partner had a difficult time understanding the concept and didn't feel my client deserved at least a 50% share of the company. With no clients, there would be no business with debt on a building, inventory, and on-going maintenance costs. Furthermore, in past negotiations for over a year, the partner kept changing his story as to how quickly he could fill orders (backlog is a deal breaker if customers had to wait longer than 90 days to receive their equipment). Another red flag was the fact that my client could never pin the guy down for specifics; his typical response was "oh, we're friends and we'll work it out—no need for lawyers and accountants."

Who will control the business?

He who owns the majority of the stock (in this case 51%) controls the company and can buy out minority shareholders at will unless specifically addressed in the company charter under a buy-sell agreement. My client was nervous if he was going to invest 100k of his money plus put his reputation on the line (he already had a 4.3 million dollar contract lined up if the partner would agree to a 50-50 stock split). Rightfully so, my client did not want to proceed with further negotiations unless his partner would budge from his majority position. In a dual owner business my bias is that the ONLY way this can work out is a 50-50 voting right and stock options whereby consensus rules (in essence each partner has veto power over any decision). Regardless of how much equity is in the business and who contributes to the equity, sweat equity must be taken into account (in my client's case, his ability to secure the business via contracts). The two need each other—without the technology, no product; without the consumer, no one to sell the product to and no income.

Survivorship

The reason for buying "key-person" insurance is to keep family members out of your business. Chances are, they don't want to be in your business anyway (unless it's a family-owned business) and the insurance pays the survivors of the deceased partner from an insurance policy equal to the percentage ownership of the business. This negates the necessity for probate and lawyers meddling into your financial affairs. It also allows the business to run smoothly. Of course, depending on how the business charter is drawn up, the surviving partner now owns 100% of the business without having to "buy out" the deceased partner's shares and preserves cash flow. Many business owners neglect this most important aspect of a business partnership which can create the most problems later on in the event of the untimely death of one of the partners. Related to this is disability insurance in the event one or both of the partners is injured and cannot perform their duties; both short and long-term disability insurance is available and major insurance carriers provide this product line.

Helpful Hints:

1. Contact your secretary of state's office and ask for an "incorporation" packet and sample forms for a charter, stock options, survivorship, and other information found in the articles of incorporation.
2. If you have a friend or family member who is partner in a business (either limited or managing), talk to them about why they incorporated the way they did—e.g. LLC, LLP, subchapter S, C-corporation?
3. Talk to an insurance agent about disability insurance, costs, and protections; also ask about "key-person" insurance.

Strategic Planning

www.planware.org is an excellent website for developing strategic and business plans for small business owners who don't have the money to hire a consultant to come and spend a few days learning the company's corporate values, branding, P&L, and human resource policies and procedures. The software template is easy to use with copy and paste capabilities as well as "writing on the fly" and frequent save features. I just completed a strategic plan for a physician primary care group practice in a few hours.

A strategic plan is not the same thing as an operational plan. Strategic planning is visionary, conceptual and directional in contrast to an operational plan which is likely to be shorter term, tactical, focused, and measurable. As an example pretend you are planning to develop a new product line. A strategic plan evaluates the market conditions and talent required given the current business climate and willingness of the organization to take up a new challenge. When Pepsi lost the "cola war" in 1996, the company wasted no time in taking on food and energy drinks that has shown double digit profits in each of the last five years. This turnaround was made possible by redefining Pepsi as a *food* and beverage company rather than just another beverage company. Before an operational business plan was developed a strategic plan looked at the current market conditions, focus groups, and predicted the health and fitness craze that defines a healthier person rather than just a younger person. This allowed Pepsi to move from the teenager market to cover the entire lifespan.

A strategic plan, unlike a business plan, is a 3-5 year look at where the company wants to be; it future-driven based on company core values and includes mission and vision statements, a SWOT analysis (strengths, weaknesses, opportunities, threats), corporate values, business objectives, key strategies, major goals, strategic action programs. A short description of each follows:

Company core values. This defines the company's core values and beliefs. To use the Pepsi example it is to provide healthier snacks and drinks that will enhance physical fitness rather than providing "empty calories" via sugars and carbs.

Mission statement. This is the central purpose of the company—its reason for doing business whether delivering a service or product.

Vision statement. This is a 3-5 year prediction of where the company wants to be. In Pepsi's case they wanted to be the leader in health drink industry with Gatorade and offer power snacks to people who want to take care of their bodies. They expanded the market from "just athletes" to the average person who wants to remain in good physical shape.

SWOT analysis. Strengths and weaknesses are *internal* to the company. This involves staffing, expertise, ancillary business solutions that define a niche that draws consumers to their products or services. Weaknesses are gaps between where the company wants to be and where they are today, sometimes defined as a "gap analysis." This is where the company's strengths are redirected to shore up the weaker areas whether it be personnel management, staff recruitment and selection, staff retention, R&D, etc. Threats and opportunities are the market conditions *external* to the company and defines the competition.

Corporate values. This is a reiteration of the company's core values and beliefs but in relationship to the consumer, shareholder, employees, trade associations, business organizations, and competing companies.

Business objectives. These can be "hard" or "soft." Hard objectives are concise descriptions that identify the responsible party, and are time-limited, focused, and measurable. Softer objectives simply state what the company needs to accomplish to close the gap between present and future goals. An example of a softer objective is that a business "will become the one entry portal for offering quality services while eliminating office overhead." A "hard" objective might be: "Over the next four years, virtual executive coaching will offer busy executives long-distance learning opportunities for business growth and expansion into new markets."

Key strategies: This is the "to do" list or action steps necessary to fulfill the objectives listed above. Examples might be: redesign of a company logo, website, joining a trade association, or building an Internet-based consumer.

Major goals. This is a list of key targets that can be achieved in the next 3-5 years. Examples might be: increasing client base by 100%, increase a new product line, spend 5% on R&D, redefine market niche, etc.

Strategic action programs. This is the "meat" in your strategic plan and defines the who, what, where, and when and builds accountability into the plan. An example might be: "ancillary healthcare staff will be recruited by a physician practice by September, 2006, to bring their expertise in vision, hearing, and weight management to increase patient referrals by 25% over the next three years and become self-sustaining profit centers to the physician practice."

Helpful Hints:

1. Go to www.planware.org and develop your own strategic plan for your current job, especially if you want to make a career move in the next 3-5 years.
2. Look at successful companies like Pepsi and find out what they did to become more diversified and profitable.
3. Hire a business coach to help you redefine how you balance career, family, spiritual, and personal life.

Running Your Small Business

Many small business owners work in a vacuum without the support of a Chamber of Commerce or trade organization. Networking, trade shows, and continuing education seminars are hard to find for niche businesses. Imagine running a Hallmark card shop and going to a business seminar on how to increase market share. First, the Hallmark shop is a franchise; secondly, branding is already your best marketing resource because you PAID to become a Hallmark shop complete with logos, standard advertising and pitches. So a marketing workshop might not be the best use of your money. However, consider the possibility that you run a small CPA firm specializing in small business development and accounting. Going to a workshop that offers different ways to incorporate, file 941s, offer employee benefits, including retirement plans might prove helpful to the business owner.

The key to running a small business as a sole proprietor is to learn to manage yourself (based on article by Peter Drucker, 1999 in *Harvard Business Review*). First, assess your strengths. What unproductive habits are preventing you from creating outcomes you desire and opportunities not seized. A SWOT (strengths, weaknesses, opportunities, and threats) can create a thumbnail picture of your internal and external factors that affect outcome and profitability. Second, how do you work? Do you process information more effectively by reading, listening to audio tapes, attending seminars, or working with others? Do you work better in the morning, after exercising, after a relaxing swim; how many work breaks do you take and how do you pace yourself? Third, what are your values? What do you envision as your most important responsibilities that create value for your company and employees? Fourth, where do you belong? Are you satisfied with a low-volume market niche with high margins; do you work best in a small company of ten or fewer employers, a sole proprietor, visionary CEO or operational COO? Select your best work style and surround yourself with staff that complements your style and values. Lastly, where can you contribute to the company? In the past, companies told their staff how to dress, when to take breaks, how to communicate and delegate, when to come to work, and demanded strict adherence to a code of ethics. Today, company loyalty is no longer a given, but a commodity to be earned and respected by your staff, with the leader setting the example.

Let's take an example and see how each of the above tenets impacts the performance of a typical small business owner. Suppose you have purchased a Midas Muffler franchise and you know nothing about the auto repair business. First, I would question why you bought the franchise in the first place, because franchises are quite risky with low profit margins and blurred geographical customer bases where competition is keen among a shrinking customer base. Mr. CEO has just borrowed 100k dollars to open a two-bay, 2500 square foot shop in an upscale suburban area. On either side of the shop is a seafood restaurant and Blockbuster video store. Parking is sufficient with good access with a turn light into the shop. A traffic analysis indicates that your light is a highly traveled area because people like to eat out and rent movies. Suppose further you are skilled at strategic planning and have put together a five-year plan to increase sales by offering more personalized service than your competition such as vending machines in the waiting room, free coffee and ice tea, internet access, *USA Today, Wall Street Journal,* and reputable magazines conducive to men and women. You also offer video games for children who might accompany their parent to replace a muffler or get a brake job. Second your working style is such that you are a cheerleader and greet your customers before they get out of their car; you introduce them to your service manager who will take personal care of them while they wait; you offer a loaner car for up to one hour if they wish not to stay while their vehicle is serviced. Third, suppose customer service is your number one company value; it's plastered on your window, decals, free pens, refrigerator magnets, and company invoices. Fourth, you belong in the front office, not micro-managing your service technicians who are managed by your service manager. You wear a nice clean white shirt with the company logo over your left breast pocket, no tie, and navy blue Dockers. Your fingernails are clean and it's clear you're the owner, not the owner-manager, not the owner-operator. Lastly, your greatest contribution to your shop is praising your employees with work incentives, tax-free gift cards, a monthly dinner at a nice restaurant for employees and their families on your expense account, and building a customer loyalty with individual service technicians by offering extra incentives for repeat customers.

I would venture to say that your shop stands a better chance of succeeding than an owner-operator shop with fewer employees, longer waits, no personal service, in a high-crime area of town. Your customer, if brave enough to leave their car at your shop for two hours, would not venture next door to rent a movie or get something to eat if the buildings on either side of your shop are abandoned with high grass surrounding poorly kept structures with broken glass and oil spills.

Helpful Hints:

1. Pick a business that interests you and write down each of your five roles described above; how will the business survive given the roles you intend to take in running the business?
2. Go into a Midas Muffler shop and notice how clean the work area and lobby are; how customer-friendly the manager is, what type of customers are attracted to the shop?
3. Pick three roles: owner, manager, and technician of a service related business and see where you are most comfortable. Ask yourself why.

Marketing New Clients

Let's face it. Most of us do not like to talk about ourselves. We prefer to talk about what we do, but if we and the doing are the same thing, then it's the "cold call" part of selling is about US. Yikes, this can be scary stuff. I'd like to offer a few tips about how to overcome your fear of marketing your business.

Tip #1: If you were sold on your business and you're an astute business person, and then think about how much easier it is to communicate this to someone else. Four years ago I heard a presentation by Ben Dean about how to transition a therapy practice into a thriving coaching practice. I was skeptical at first and only took the workshop to gain some CEUs for my therapy practice. But Ben's enthusiasm and that of the group convinced me that coaching was possible and people would pay to be coached by phone. Next time you tell someone about yourself, remember that you've already sold your most skeptical client—YOU.

Tip #2: Practice your elevator speech until it becomes second nature. That means you have two minutes to "pitch" what you do to a complete stranger. Establish eye contact, talk slowly, and make sure you get the person's business card and email address; if they don't have one on them, make sure you give them yours by first asking permission. Make sure your email address is on your card.

Tip #3: Forget brochures and postcards for initial contacts. These forms of marketing are better suited for presentations and workshops. Always carry your business cards with you and look for opportunities to talk about what you do, even when you're on vacation.

Tip #4: Think of yourself as an ambassador of good will. I know a disabled vet who is on disability but he gives out business cards with the message "Expect a Miracle" on them. That's it—no phone number, no picture, and no email address. The message is simple, but very powerful. When you direct your message at offering something of value to a prospective customer then your focus shifts from you to them. This is called "service marketing" in some circles but the impact is to remove the pressure from selling yourself to *giving* something away.

Tip #5: Marketing is not selling; it's putting you out as a unique resource. Whether you've got a paint company, car dealership, or consulting practice, you must find a market niche that defines you as distinct. We have a furniture salesman in Houston, Texas who is successful because he offers same day delivery on any purchase, with no back orders. How many of his competitors can do this? In your business, can you deliver the goods promptly with no returns?

Tip #6: Look at potential customers as future marketing associates. If you land a contract and do a good job for someone, then your satisfied customer will market for you. The reverse is also true, so be careful.

Tip #7: Don't leave your marketing to a consultant or ad firm. No one knows your product or service better than you. If you don't have the time to generate new business then you should not be in business for yourself.

Tip #8: Electronic advertising is great, but do you have what it takes to "close the sale?" This tip is for those who expect to derive passive income from a web-based business. Be prepared to spend $5 to $10 thousand on a site that has the right meta tags and search engines. And once you accomplish this, remember that you still end up talking to someone on the phone before they decide on your product or service.

Tip #9: Marketing is costly, but necessary. I'm not talking dollars, necessarily, but being prepared for opportunities that may present themselves as interruptions. If you promise to deliver information or a product within a certain timeframe, you'd better do it. Trust is paramount. You typically have only one chance to deliver so make it count.

Tip #10: Be passionate about what you do. This is the most important and that's why I saved it for last. You can have the greatest business or marketing plan, but if you don't live it everyday, then others will not resonate to your product or service.

A quick story: I was on the elevator (literally) going up to my office on the 6th floor of a bank building in Houston with a smile on my face. The person next to me was a bank officer I'd met in passing a month before and given him my business card. He indicated that he was hoping to find me in, because he wanted to talk to me since our initial meeting. Long story short, he had a wedding video business in college that was quite successful that he had to put on the back burner while pursuing his banking career. I typically allow an hour before my first client to get my charts in order and review the clients scheduled for that day. Instead of "putting this guy off" we opened up the office together, made some coffee, and I listened to what he wanted from coaching. I did absolutely nothing except be available at his moment and become an active listener. He's now a client and we start this month.

Helpful Hints:

1. Next time you're out running errands alone look to help someone by giving them some free information. Last time I had my oil changed, I was sitting in the waiting room and noticed a lady looking through the yellow pages for a dentist.
2. Remember to smile and look up when you are alone. Who wants to do business with a sour face who looks down at the floor?
3. Look for a surprise each and every day. You may not experience one on that day but you WILL be surprised. Happy people are attracted to happy people.

Tolerating Instability and Uncertainty

This chapter features challenges facing executive coaches who coach entrepreneurs. The first three challenges discussed in previous newsletters included: perceiving the need for change, moving towards commitment and planning, and accepting the pace of change.

Given the fast pace that changes take place discussed in last month's newsletter, it's only natural that instability and uncertainty can lead to regressing to "the good old days" when status quo meant "don't make any waves." Work load in vertical bureaucracies that focus on procedure and "doing it right" tends to take on a life of its own. The recent two hurricane disasters with Katrina and Rita and the FEMA's ineffectiveness to deliver needed help to families and small businesses in New Orleans is a case in point in getting bogged down in red tape and miscommunication between federal, state, and local levels. Without getting into the blame game, suffice it to say that only two small businesses were helped within the first thirty days *after* applying for a small business loan (*Fortune Small Business*, October, 2005). Many of the supplies delivered to families were generously donated by individuals and local governments, as evidenced by the city of Houston offering shelter, clothing, and food.

Let's take the above scenario and offer a hypothetical entrepreneurial intervention to the hurricane refugees mentioned above. Suppose Wal-Mart provided food and household items for the crisis intervention teams responding to the hurricane victims. Half of their stores had suffered sufficient damage and electrical outages that the food would soon become spoiled anyway. Why not give the food to the relief workers and victims who had electricity; or perhaps offer the food and hardware items to a cooperative housing project that provided rent subsidies to those left homeless. For a brief period of weeks, this is *exactly* what happened in several Gulf Coast communities. Wal-Mart employees began offering items without the bureaucratic red tape of getting approval from the top. This was made possible by the astute Wal-Mart leadership that had already gone into an entrepreneurial mode to assist their store managers and employees.

Although there were service disruptions in the daily operations of many large and small businesses, professional management knew to let their store managers make executive decisions without micromanaging by policies and procedures. There are untold stories of small business owners reaching out to the victims. People in Houston and other Gulf Coast communities emptied their refrigerators and brought food and gasoline to the victims stranded on the highways in the largest metropolitan evacuation in history as two million Houstonians took to the highways to escape Rita's wrath. Although there were some mishaps as far as opening up highways and having gasoline trucks ready for stranded motorists, the mayor, governor, and FEMA did a remarkable job, having learned from the mishaps in New Orleans.

The point is this—entrepreneurial spirit is like a "strike force team" that can attack the problem quickly, effectively, and efficiently, precisely because there are no standing policies and procedures and multiple, vertical levels of jurisdiction and turf protection. This is not to say that entrepreneurs don't operate without a vision, strategy, and business plan. But entrepreneurs can tolerate uncertainty and disruptions and change course quickly to meet a crisis or develop a new product line. It's the willingness and ability to take calculated risks in the face of uncertainty and doubt.

Helpful Hints:

1. Pick up your local newspaper and go to the city and state section. Look to see how a local business responded to crisis.

2. Look at the business section of your local paper and see what local businesses are offering the community in the way of information, financial assistance, and volunteers.
3. Ask your company what their policy is regarding time off to help your family in time of crisis without evoking the Family and Medical Leave Act (FMLA).

Working Towards Resolution vs. Fragmentation

In prior chapters we touched on four challenges for entrepreneurs: perceiving the need to change versus denial and isolation, moving toward commitment and planning versus indecision and procrastination, accepting the pace of change versus doubt and uncertainty, and tolerating instability and uncertainty versus regressing to old ways. Now we will focus on "working towards resolution versus fragmentation."

Even as organizations change they maintain core values and beliefs. Surviving a transition, introducing a new product or service, realignment of function and priorities all seek to integrate the old with the new. We don't "throw out the baby with the bathwater" in bringing change to organizations. The challenge for the entrepreneur in this step is to stabilize the organization around an innovative, integrated way of doing business. The alternative to integration is conflict and fragmentation with various departments and people operating in opposing ways in "turf battles."

As a way to introduce this next challenge to entrepreneurs, I've decided on an exciting development of "shareware" versus proprietary software which is sold by major software companies. There is a battle developing between copyrighted software companies and game developers who unabashedly and shamelessly place their games on the Internet for free downloads. This "sharing the technology" approach is being picked up by our younger generation interested in flash presentations, video streaming, graphic design, and web page development. Many existing Internet sites offer free downloads for strategic planning (planware.org) and interpersonal growth (authentichappiness.org).

Dr. Keith Barton

The software industry is in transition from proprietary "off the shelf" programs to more dynamic software that can be tailored to specific companies and problems. The Linux system is an example of using an operating system without spending hundreds of dollars. My view is that we will see a friendlier shareware that operates on "point and drag" technology to simplify and personalize our working on the Internet. Self-help books will be replaced by "self-help shareware" that informs, educates, and increases productivity.

The challenge for entrepreneurs is how to survive in a "non-competitive" environment that markets "ideas" rather than technology. Legal issues will undoubtedly ensue around trademark, copyright, and public vs. private domain. Let's take as an example the latest proprietary game from Microsoft, the XBOX 360, which was sold out last week but some gaming units are being returned for "glitches" in the software that freeze the video. We've also experienced viruses that are susceptible to proprietary products and systems that do not exist on more user friendly systems such as "Mambo."

The challenge for program developers during the next five years will be to increase market share and product identity while building a corporate culture that moves from maverick to competitive to stay in business. We're all away of "loss leaders' in retail stores—those sale items that bring people into the store, only to find the product sold out but can purchase a more expensive item. This will happen in the shareware industry if shareware is to survive and maintain corporate identity—just witness the phenomenal success of Google and Yahoo. Search engines that increase traffic to WebPages is still in its infancy and further refinements and tools will assist the Internet surfer in obtaining more relevant information with the pinpoint accuracy of "smart bombs." Another development on the horizon is collaboration between software developers who pool talent and resources to bring R&D products to the general public in pre-release, Beta versions. This will assist developers in feedback in a competitive marketplace rather than secret, proprietary shops across the country.

And now, for my most controversial prediction: that money will cease to be the driving force behind software innovation; the new mantra will be one of product volume in a user-friendly environment. Product Identification (Branding) will be the next wave, much like Google and Yahoo were in the 90s. We will see new companies and IPOs around user friendly technology that operates in a maverick, fast-pace environment that avoids fragmentation because there is no "turf" to protect. The value placed on these companies will depend on user demand, and companies will be bought and sold based on "innovation" rather than "technology."

Helpful Hints:

1. Surf the net and see what free shareware you can find.
2. Read the story behind Google and Yahoo; there are many excellent articles and books on this subject; look through your local bookstore or visit Amazon.com.
3. Free WebPages exist on the Internet. You don't need to spend money to have a personalized presence in Cyberspace. Many Web Designers use free templates from various shareware programs, like Mambo.

Practical Ways of Managing Trust

Robert Hurley in the *HBR* September 2006 issue has written an interesting article about the mental calculations we make before trusting someone else. He estimates that about half of all managers in corporate America don't trust their leaders. This is an amazing statistic, if found true, because the trust issue speaks to loyalty and values. Whether one is deep in a hostile takeover, friendly merger, bringing a new product to market, or introducing the next patent or trademark, trust is critical to the success of corporate culture. Think back a few years when Ken Lay told his employees that they had nothing to fear; in fact, buy more Enron he told them (as he and his executive staff dumped their stock).

With outsourcing, age discrimination, paranoia around new products, internet security, and securities fraud common to our corporate environments today, it's no surprise that employees are looking over their shoulders, not sharing information, and maintaining status quo to keep a low profile. This bunker mentality tanks employee morale and leaves employees fearful and anxious. How much teamwork does one imagine will take place under these conditions?

Hurley posits decision-maker and situational factors that influence trust along a continuum. Higher trust is predicated on more risk tolerance of the decision-maker, along with better emotional adjustment and relative power he or she may have. Regarding situational factors increased trust is correlated with: the security each party feels, the similarities between them, how well aligned their interests, showing benevolent concern, leadership capability, and good communication.

For those managers showing low risk tolerance, leaders should spend more time explaining options and risks while offering some sort of safety net. An example might be offering more 401k options from conservative to more volatile investment strategies that factor in income averaging and portfolio diversity. Those leaders who publicly recognize manager achievements are more likely to be trusted. Leaders should act more like mentors and coaches than dictatorial figureheads. Emphasis on common values such as employee safety, consumer satisfaction, and branding of staff also increases trust between managers and leaders. Focusing on strategy, vision, and goals brings a long-term perspective and puts managers at ease rather than quarterly profits and quotas that breed competition and rivalries. Above all, be fair with your managers. Don't show favoritism and lead by example. There's nothing more debilitating than giving plum assignments and insider information to the same managers. It's sure to foster resentment among the remaining managers. Pairing less experienced managers with more experienced mentors fosters knowledge transfer and trust rather than the "boot camp" approach where junior managers are "put to the test" as if it were a fraternity or sorority initiation. Another approach is to promise less and deliver more. This gives managers a comfort zone from which to operate while at the same time tolerating more risk in future assignments. Finally, successful leaders are human and share their mistakes with staff in a constructive way that invites risk-taking behaviors while personal competence is deemphasized.

Unconditional loyalty in corporations is a relic that has outlived its usefulness, because managers expect more from their leaders. Charisma may land a job for top leaders but their performance is measured by the way they conduct themselves in good times and bad times. Nine-eleven was a testament to the mayor's leadership which led to heroic efforts on the part of New York firemen and police officers. Rudy Giuliani showed courage under fire as he walked the streets of lower Manhattan giving encouragement to all emergency response personnel who risked their lives to minimize loss of human life.

Helpful Hints:

1. Pick a successful company and do a psychological profile on its CEO. What leadership qualities are apparent and in what situations?

2. On your next 360 evaluation discuss with your staff how much they trust you and have them provide examples to support their assessments.
3. Tape record your next talk with your staff and count the number of times the word "we" is used instead of the word "I."

Accepting the Pace of Change

Accepting the pace of change is another challenge facing entrepreneurs; last chapter we talked about moving towards commitment and planning and the prior month we discussed perceiving the need for change versus denial and isolation.

Coaching entrepreneurs requires energy, building and maintaining momentum and making the right decisions at the right times. I call it "coaching on steroids" because you may get a call at three in the morning from London or New York from a stressed-out CEO who has a board presentation the next morning without a clue of what and how to present a change of direction for his or her company. You better grab a cup of java and pen and start writing because your CEO will be talking non-stop at a rapid-fire pace. You may think he's bipolar but his passion and energy will physically and emotionally drain you if you let it. Your job as coach is to maintain the CEO's momentum but clearly steer him or her to shorter-term objectives for tomorrow's meeting—e.g. vision, internal scan of resources, external scan of competition and challenges, operational plans, best, worst and most likely case scenarios, integration of management with the Board and most importantly, a knowledge of group dynamics that will make or break the CEO's presentation.

CEOs who argue for rapid change will face the "old guard" who want to maintain the status quo (the old NIMC syndrome—Not In My Company). Lower management may become frustrated because their roles and jobs will change and they become anxious thereby creating a work slowdown. The Board may want a "hands on" stake in the company and want to micro-manage the executive staff. The CEO must become a "buffer" if this happens to protect his staff from board interference and working for the Board instead of the CEO. If this happens the CEO is most likely on his/her way out the door and look for an interim CEO or a board member to step in the management role.

Process skills required of the coach included: deep listening (both actual and perceived). In the coaching community, this is called Level IV listening or "seamless listening" whereby the coach and CEO become hand and glove in supporting the CEO in process skill development. This includes critical reflectivity to test the CEO's assumptions and perceptions about his/her relationship with the Board. The coach is NOT to recommend topics, make interpretations, or control content with the CEO. The coach's job is to set up dynamics for the CEO's board presentation. These include: mapping, review and analysis, document areas for change and improvement, set the stage, devise action steps, implement, measure performance, troubleshoot, evaluate outcomes, and devise required adjustments. Let's look at each of these briefly: (From Randi Smith, Ph.D., PCC, and Principal, Virtual Group Institute, LLC, 2005).

Mapping: Integration of the mission statement with the internal and external scan to create a list of critical success factors (CSFs).

Review and Analysis: Does the mission track with the vision; will each CSF remain critical during the proposed change?

Document Analysis: The "gap" between the current and desired outcome is documented for each CSF.

Set the Stage: Organizational, group, and individual roles and responsibilities are defined during the plan implementation.

Devise Action Steps: Human and other resources, measurement criteria, timeframes, and cost are defined for each action plan objective.

Implement: Implementation is carefully guided and interim results are evaluated as produced.

Measure Performance: Documented processes for ongoing performance leads to one of two conclusions: the interim results are acceptable and implementation of the strategic plan should continue OR the interim results are unacceptable and Troubleshooting is required.

Troubleshooting: the CEO helps his Board brainstorm alternative actions (options) and make a good decision about adjust the action plan.

Evaluate Outcomes: Are the results what was desired?

Devise Required Adjustments: The Board brainstorms as opposed to affixing blame on the CEO or going into catharsis about corporate management.

Now don't freak out and assume the coach addresses each of the above ten points with his or her CEO in distress at three in the morning. Coaching entrepreneurs requires the ability to "dance in the moment" with your CEO and work with him/her in recognizing the above steps and how to work with one's Board in working towards planned change that will ultimately have the Board's "buy-in" and approval. Once the CEO has Board approval then the same process can be repeated with the CEO's executive staff to build *esprit de corps* and the chances of a successful planned change.

Helpful Hints:

1. Develop a vision statement for your coaching practice to see if it conveys a clear message; if not, rework it until it is clear and crisp.
2. Develop an external scan for your coaching practice to see your coaching niche is defined by market conditions and potential customers.
3. Develop and internal scan for your coaching practice that defines financial and training/development objectives. Possible factors might include: your level of confidence in your coaching, capability assessment, personal expectations, interests and passions, time perception, etc.

Managing Middlescence

The following summary is taken from the March, 2006 issue of *HBR* to help companies identify and rekindle opportunities and motivation of mid-level managers known as "B" players.

We've all heard the term "obsolescence" to define the failure of one's skills to keep up with the fast-pace changing technology and leadership tools necessary to manage and motivate people. But with the Boomers now approaching their mid-fifties a new term has emerged—middlesence—to define burn-out, bottlenecked, and bored "B" players who are below star "A" material but essential to the company. With longer life spans and fewer severance packages available for "B" players they are faced with anxiety and fear of keeping a job that they no longer enjoy but are afraid to leave because they won't be hired in their fifties by another company. The sources of frustration are many but here are a few:

Career bottleneck: The Boomers are large and too many people are competing for too few leadership positions in companies. Next to job security this is the biggest concern of managers in their 40s and 50s.

Work/life tension: Medicare workers are caught between commitments to children and families at the same time their work responsibilities are increasing.

Lengthening horizon: The Boomers are not the savers their parents were and they face working longer to maintain health benefits and maintain their standard of living.

Skills obsolescence: We've talked about this before; at a time when mid-career employees need rejuvenation, companies typically cut back on leadership development programs.

Disillusionment with employer: This has to do with the wide disparity in compensation between the "A" players (VPs, executive staff) and the rest of the players. Also mergers, acquisitions, downsizing, and resizing have created distrust in the ranks.

Burnout: People who have been giving their lives to the company for 20 years are stressed and stretched, often finding their work repetitive and tiresome.

Career disappointment: Reality sets in after 20 years that our youthful vigor and ideals are not being realized or co-opted by our desire to just hold on.

The gist of the *HBR* article by Robert Morison, Tamara Erickson, and Ken Dychtwald is that companies are ill-prepared to manage middlesence because it is so pervasive, invisible, and culturally uncharted. The authors offer three strategies for revitalizing careers:

1. *Remove the barriers to upward or lateral mobility by relaxing some of the company's policies and procedures.*
2. *Find the keepers just below your star "A" players and give them the special attention already provided to the star players. Send them to a management seminar for a week at a Business School that offers a more relaxed, campus environment.*
3. *Offer fresh assignments in a different geographical location or part of the organization. Bill Gates offered four top game designers an unlimited budget and their own off-campus location to develop the XBOX 360 over a four-year duration.*

Helpful Hints:

1. Develop your career path for the next five years; what obstacles and opportunities do you see?
2. Find a mentor in your company who will coach you.
3. Take management courses whenever possible: online, local college, via your company.

Employee Turnover

Employee turnover is a nightmare for managers who must bear the cost of retraining new hires. According to the January issue of *Fortune*, the top five reasons given for leaving a job are: better compensation and benefits, better career opportunity, ready for a new experience, dissatisfied with career opportunities at present job, and desire to change careers or industries. A recent poll indicated that 75% of managers persistently worry about good people leaving; this is coupled with the fact that unemployment is at a low 4.5% making it more difficult to find qualified people to replace your "star" employees.

Battling turnover takes more creativity today because more employees are taking matters into their own hands and creating their own opportunities. The authors labeled five potential candidates for turnover: the Techie, the Mom, the Vet, the MBA, and the Part-timer. While stereotypical in some respects these qualities represent the upward mobility climbers who want to take charge of their careers instead of relying on inside job postings in HR. Let's take a closer look at each of our potential candidates looking for more depth and flexibility.

The Technie: This person loves gadgets and prefers mobile computing. Cubicles are a thing of the past; no time clocks, no face to face meetings, no parking fees or enduring commutes. These folks literally work at home or "on the fly." With IPOD, Blackberry, and cell phone in hand plus broadband connectivity they can sit in on meetings anywhere in the world, tackle problems, and talk to other key players from their home, airport, or car. *Capital One* rolled out their Future of Work in October, 2006 and placed 4000 iPODs in their employees' hands to download any of 10,000 different courses from distance learning programs, many from top Ivy League business schools. No more hotel rooms, rental cars, and boring meeting rooms. The Technie can set his/her own schedule and work hours convenient to their personal lives. The nine to five job has become obsolete when considering time zones and the rapidity of decisions made across flatter levels within the company. The flexibility helps with solitude when one needs to focus and collaborate with others.

The Vet: Companies rely too much on HR to handle employee complaints. You can have the best managers in the world but the company won't prosper if the worker bees are not consulted about why they're dissatisfied with their jobs. Forget surveys; people will not be honest fearing reprisals and believe their comments won't be used in the annual report with all the fancy graphics and statistics. *Quad Graphics* is a printing plant in Martinsburg, Virginia. In mid-2005, Quad realized that employee satisfaction was dependent on the local economy and leisure activities available in that particular plant location. A veteran talent specialist, Bill Klingelsmith was hired (among other vets) to hold on to workers in their markets. In the Martinsville plant, NASCAR racing is a big weekend activity and folks will drive five hundred miles to attend a race. Bill also noticed that employees liked to work on their own cars. So he started handing out his card at local car shows and NASCAR races, and turnover decreased 30%. Employee retention is not only about money and working conditions. It's about talking with the front-line worker to see what they enjoy doing with their families when they're NOT working for you.

The Mom: As part of *Deloitte's* Personal Pursuits Program, Tina Swenson, a tax manager, is on a five-year sabbatical to raise her daughter. Deloitte pays for her AICPA license and training courses and will rehire her when she's ready. *Deloitte's* in-house study found that 62% of women who graduated from top business schools leave the corporate world after their second child. Even with parental leave, reduced work hours, and on-site daycare, Deloitte was still losing top female talent to motherhood. Since beginning the Pursuit Program, the difference between male and female turnover results has gone from 7% to zero.

The MBA: Julian Duncan is an assistant brand manager for *Nike*. He enrolled in *Nike's* intensive management training program which rotates him through six marketing assignments is 24 months. The rotations expose Duncan to higher-ups who can help him navigate the corporate culture. He conversed with *Nike* co-founder Phil Knight in the cafeteria and emailed a VP with a question who gave the young MBA 30 minutes of face to face time. The *Nike* culture is to encourage employees to plot their own courses. They want "go getters" who aren't afraid to ask questions and learn from senior management.

The Part-timer: Brenda Fung is an intranet web designer who has worked at *First Horizon*, a financial services firm for 13 years. She wanted to scale back to a 28-hour workweek in four 7-hour days to pursue more time with her family. She still receives the same medical, dental, life insurance, and retirement benefits she got as a full-time employee. The part-time program is called Prime Time with 90 employees currently enrolled and turnover has decreased significantly.

These innovative companies spent millions recruiting and hiring top talent and they want to retain their "star" players who will continue to benefit the company. Employee retention has not received its long overdue attention in part because companies thought their hands were tied when employees left to join the competition. Innovative programs such as those presented by Anne Fisher in *Fortune's* February, 2007, issue are a testament to the old adage once coined by legendary football coach, Darrell K. Royal, when asked who he would start for UT in the National Championship game in 1969 against Notre Dame: his reply was "we're going to dance with who brung (sic) us," a reference that he would go with his starting quarterback, James Street, who made it happen all season for the Longhorns.

Helpful Hints:

1. At your next exit interview with your employee ask them what you could have done to make them feel more a part of the company.
2. Ask your longest-term employee why they still work for you. What would have made them leave earlier?
3. Give each employee a voucher toward a piece of art to place in their cubicle or office, compliments of the company.

Managing Your Business in a Downturn

I think everyone will agree that 2008 will be a downturn in the U.S. economy; whether the downturn will meet the economic definition of recession of a decline in Gross Domestic Product (GDP) for at least two consecutive quarters. Worst-case scenario is that we will not pull out of a recession for two more years. Most-likely case scenario is that 2008 will be a challenging year for small business. As the number of jobs continue to go overseas, tax credits continue to be offered to the large corporations, and capital gains taxes remain above thirty percent, small business owners will struggle to maintain annual production goals, despite decreased daily cash flow for running their companies. In *Fortune* magazine, Ray Charan offers an interesting formula for making your company better in our current downtown.

Keep building. Do not panic, but instead refocus your energy on what made your company successful in the first place. Was it customer service? A new gadget? Easier access? More variety? He quotes what CEO Ray Gilmartin did when *Merck* was losing many of its Brand name patents and the fall out from the *Vioxx* scandal. He elected to increase R&D spending from 12% to 20% from 1999 to 2004. For *Merck* its core value was finding new drugs to make people live longer and enjoy a better quality of life. (Go to *Fortune*, pages 94-98 to see how *Merck* went from Scandal to Stardom). He also continued bonuses for those stellar employees running the larger profit centers within the company. One of the surest ways to lose talent is to cut pay and bonuses across the board in down times. This punishes everyone for outside threats (like litigation) that affect the bottom line.

Communicate intensely. When the economy slows, intra-company communication should speed up. Many CEOs insulate themselves from their workforce and customers. What *EMC²* did after its stock price plummeted 90% was reconfigure their business strategy after conducting focus groups, town hall meetings, and intranet letters to query not only their customers, but their customer's customers. When facts or economic conditions change so must your business strategy, to paraphrase a leading historical economist, Keynes. Too many companies continue the same ole' same ole', keeping their heads in the sand, praying that macroeconomics and government subsidies will turn them around.

Evaluate your customers. During downturns, you should identify your higher-risk, cash-poor customers. Don't continue to supply customers who haven't paid you in four months. Cut them off! Find new markets for your products; help finance your customers with short-term loans or let them buy in smaller quantities. Cut out the middle man and try selling direct to your customers over the Internet. This is what made *eBay* so successful.

No across-the-board cuts. Prune, don't cut down the entire bush. *Procter and Gamble* did this in the late 1990s by dropping stagnant brands like *Comet* and *Crisco* and focusing more on environmental-friendly products for the household. Detroit automakers continue to produce giant SUVs despite high gas prices with lower profit margins per vehicle when they should have invested in smaller hybrids like *Toyota* has done. The American consumer hasn't caught on but they will when gas prices move above $4 a gallon. People are now reconsidering jobs that require two hour commutes.

So what kind of CEO do you want in 2008? Do you want the ostridge or owl? Good business sense relies on more that internal knowledge of one's company and "doing business." A strong company remains strong during the downturns—they learn when to "batten down the hatches" and prepare for bad times by slicing and selling off their liabilities (money losers) and building and shoring up their bread and butter. Getting back to basics is key to a successful ride through turbulent waters and you want a CEO with a vision and knowledge of global macroeconomics to weather the storm.

Helpful Hints:

1. Research other companies besides *P&G* and *Merck* who changed business strategy to survive tough times.
2. If you're a business owner, how often do you talk to your customers as to what they really need and appreciate about your business?
3. Despite the ups and downs in our economy as evidenced by the stock market during the past forty years, the overall trend is 6% post-inflation and taxes.

Net Promoter Score (NPS)

It's not a new TV or cable network. Small businesses are turning to customer satisfaction and rewarding employees for their NPS scores. It's s single number that can fluctuate depending on your interactions with customers. NPS was first introduced by Fred Reichheld, a partner at Boston consulting firm, Bain & Co. According to Bain's research a company's promoters are responsible for 80% or more of new customer referrals, which is key to increasing revenue.

Here's how NPS works. First, ask your customers to rate you on 0-10 scale on the question: "How likely is it that you would recommend this company to a friend or colleague?" Then sort the responses into three groups: promoters (9-10), passives (7-8), and detractors (0-6). The percentage of promoters minus detractors equals your score; thus, a company with 75% promoters and 15% detractors would have an NPS of 60.

According to Reichheld the average U.S. company has an NPS of 15. Scores above 50 are really great. Rewarding employees based on their NPS scores creates an incentive for better customer service which is really the edge in consumer-driven industries such as tanning salons, resort and hotel stays, food service, phone answering services and messaging systems, tutoring—just about any service directed towards the customer with no middle man. Ken Gibson, Learning Rx founder that helps clients improve their memory, linked NPS scores to bonuses; those staff who received a score of 90 or better received a bonus of 20% of their annual salary. Those with scores 70-90 received a 10% bonus, and those less than 70, nothing.

Software giant Intuit also uses NPS by getting their detractors to join forums to get more out of their software by speaking directly with the software designers rather than a "customer service" specialist in another country. NPS creates a demand for networking results by customers providing marketing for the company. Hotel.com has done this for years using a five star rating system for hotel stays in different service areas: room, restaurant, lounge, pool, housekeeping, gym, etc. Movies have been rated that influence consumer demand. Just about any product or service can be rated; the key is to encourage your end users (the consumer) to rate the service without inducements or bias.

Your highest customer referral sources can also be rewarded with company merchandise such as t-shirts, software, name recognition on websites and blogs. Betsy Weber, is chief evangelist for Techsmith based in Okemos, Michigan, which makes Camtasia Studio, a kind of VCR for your PC capable of recording a sequence of screen shots. Tangerine Wellness offers weight-loss programs to employees of big corporations. For increased referrals from Rockford, another company, Tangerine pitches prospects on Rockford's ATV and motor home business. There are no monetary incentives, only cross-referrals.

The NPS also borrows from a concept used several years ago called "Service Marketing" whereby the service is more important than the product. Call centers can be laborious and impersonal. If a knowledgeable PC engineer were to answer your call (rather than a contract person who knows little about the product), then customers would be more willing to rate the help desk more positively. Knowledge plus service = consumer satisfaction and increased referrals. The link is even more direct in service industries where the consumer receives a direct benefit—e.g. salons, health clubs, hotels, ticketing, baggage, personal assistants. It's not who you *know* but who you *please*.

* From Justin Martin's article in *Fortune Small Business*, "Get Customers to Sell for You."

Helpful Hints:

1. Compute your own NPS score and tie to employee incentives and see if revenues increase over the next year.
2. Use employee questionnaires online such as "Survey Monkey" and post results on your website.
3. Ask customers if they would be willing to participate in the one NPS question and give them a store credit or online credit.

Section Two: Personality and Cognitive Learning Styles

Section Two relates to cognitive and personality characteristics necessary to running a successful business. Not everyone is cut out to run their own shop. The lessons learned in section one only position oneself for running their business; thus, section one relates to the structuring of a small business. Without the emotional, cognitive, and relational competence, your business will fail because you neglected to incorporate the knowledge, skills, and abilitities learned in business school with the psychological correlates of successfully leading and managing your business. Topics in section two speak to: the alpha male, the destructive power of overachievers, coaching entrepreneurs, perceiving he need for change, moving towards planning and commitment, reintroducing entrepreneurialism, personality vs. cognitive learning styles, Gregorc learning styles, emotional competence, CMOs, and crazy bosses.

The Alpha Male

Kate Ludeman and Ernie Erlandson, both executive coaches in Austin have written a fascinating book, entitled the *Alpha Male Syndrome*, published by Harvard University Press in 2006. This book is a must read for anyone coaching executives. The authors themselves are typical of the executives they surveyed. Kate is an industrial psychologist and coach; her husband is a retired cardiovascular surgeon and now executive coach. They suggest four subtypes of alpha male (and female) executives: the Commander, the Visionary, the Strategist, and the Executor. Each has his/her own strengths and limitations. A short description of each follows:

The Commander: Decisive, strong, and authoritative; exudes confidence; often charismatic; has a big appetite for achievement and thirst for victory; brings out the best in others (think George S. Patton). Risk to the organization involves: sole player; domineering and intimidating; argues to win point; generates fear and self-protective culture; competes with peers; envious; loose with the rules (think Andrew Fastow).

The Visionary: High standards and expansive goals; inspires with view of future; makes creative leaps; strong convictions; unwavering faith, and tenacious will; trusts instincts (think Michael Dell); risk to organization involves overconfident about ideas; excessive bravado; defensive when challenged; closed to input; ignores reality, losing support of pragmatists; spins the truth (think Ken Lay).

The Strategist: Quick, probing mind; objective, analytic, data-driven, methodical; sees underlying patterns; leaps beyond the obvious and integrates disparate ideas (think Bill Bellichek, coach of the New England Patriots); risk to the organization involves: opinionated know-it-all; smug, arrogant, pretentious; has to be right; can't admit mistakes; cold and unemotional; lacks team spirit; disconnects from others (think Jeff Skilling).

The Executor: disciplined, tireless pursuit of results; uncanny eye for spotting problems; gives excellent feedback and wake-up calls; moves people to action; helps team grow (think Omar Bradley). Risk to the organization: sets unreasonable expectations; micromanages; prone to workaholism and burning out employees; impatient; overly critical; focuses on shortcomings; expresses displeasure, not appreciation (think Jimmy Carter).

The authors offer a self-test for anyone who leads a company or coaches a CEO. The alpha "triangle" involves villain, victim, and hero roles for those who push the limits of their leadership. Commander villains demand extreme loyalty and subservience (think George Bush). Visionary villains believe in a bright shining future that no one else can even glimpse (think Al Gore). Strategist villains are intellectual bullies who think they have all the answers (think Bill O'Reilly). Executor villains are irritating nags, constantly looking over everyone's shoulder (think your own boss).

Alpha "victims" include: accommodator, complainer, conflict avoider, overwhelmed, poor me, procrastinator, resigned to whatever, and worrywart. Alpha "heroes" include: cheerleader, energizer bunny, flatterer, harmonizer, peacemaker, protector, rescuer, and trooper.

Fully half of the Commanders also have anger, competitiveness, and impatience. Heart attacks and other stress-related diseases are part of the risk factors with alpha commanders. Female commanders are more subtle with their anger and competitive edges, and cloak their anger with more passive-aggressive tactics—e.g. letting a committee recommendation die a slow death. Visionaries can be so far out of the mainstream of the organization, that they can rile everyone into a frenzy with the myriad, random, and disorganized ideas they come up with, expecting staff to execute on every idea with staff burnout a surety. Strategists can be so painstakingly unemotional that people are treated as cogs in a wheel. This John Wayne approach to managing is like sending the first wave of troops up the side of the hill at Iwo Jima. Executors can be such micromanagers that no one wants to take on assignments for fear of second-guessing.

The Alpha Male Team (or high performance team) is discussed in terms of coaching groups of alpha males and females who must work together to reach a common goal. Pitfalls abound without an astute group process coach who can pick up on the nuances of group behavior. Clearing the air of anger, resentment, and hostility are key to keeping a group on task. Other tools include healthy competition that places the needs of the group above individual egos; collaboration is another useful tool to build consensus. Opening yourself to feedback and contrary opinions leads to self-disclosure and a level playing field without executive titles and roles.

Helpful Hints:

1. Take the Alpha Test in Ludeman and Erlandson's book to see what subtype alpha male or female you are. What do you want to change about your behavior to be more convincing and genuine to staff and peers?
2. Look at the Apprentice show on TV. What alpha type does Donald Trump epitomize? What group dynamic does he encourage for one to be successful?
3. Pick a successful company who was in Fortune 100's fastest growing companies and look for alpha subtypes that complement one another.

The Destructive Power of Overachievers

You've seen the type—always the first to arrive and the last one to leave. These folks have total 24-7 connectivity to the office with the latest techie gadget. They walk around with Blackberries in their ears while sipping on a Cappuccino with the *Wall Street Journal* folded under their arm. They talk 90 mph, interrupt others, hog conversations, and always seem to be on the "cutting edge." What you don't see is their insecurities, doctor bills, broken relationships, lack of social life, and few friendships. Scott Spreier, Mary Fontaine, and Ruth Malloy in their article, "Leadership Run Amok" in the *HBR* June, 2006, issue describe six styles of leadership that leaders use to motivate, develop, and direct their employees: *directive, visionary, affiliative, participative, pacesetting, and coaching.* They studied 21 senior managers at IBM with responsibility for large global accounts and multimillion dollar revenue accounts. They found that strong, aggressive leaders relied on achievement motives and were visionary, affiliative, participative, and coaches to their direct reports. In contrast to assertive leaders, neutral or demotivating climates also used achievement motives to meet targets but their primary leadership style was pacesetting. The "pacesetter" uses leadership by example; they set high standards for themselves. It is a typical "go-to" style for overachievers but only works in short-term, crisis environments. Coaching, on the other hand, works better in long-term, lower stress situations where continuity and cross-training are important to the organization.

Gone are the days of the "John Wayne" heroics in management. You've seen this pacesetter. He or she is given the reins to achieve a short-term goal, typically cost cutting prior to a merger or selling off assets. They ride herd on direct reports with the finesse of a hand grenade hurled into Monday morning's meeting. These leaders do not care about participative management, making friends, having a personal or social life. Their marching orders come directly from the Board of Directors and this "take no prisoners" managerial approach creates confusion that keeps direct reports in a frenzy until they crash and burn. Ross Perot at EDI and Jack Welch before he retired from GE are the paragons of this approach. These leaders are intelligent, charismatic, charming, and can politic with the best.

But today's corporations are multinational and incorporate different cultures and decision-making styles. Imagine the President of SONY kicking butt to increase market share taken over by Samsung. A softer, coaching style is more suited to the business climate of the 21st Century and Spreier et al found that the coaching style increased by 17% at IBM over the past several years, while the pacesetting style decreased by 5%. Collaboration and teamwork replaced heroics, although IBM executives remained high achievers. In other words *process* is key, not *product*. Group culture remains a powerful tool against overachievers and the results from sociological research of industrial plants in the 1900s still rings true today—no one likes a "rate buster." Peer group pressure has been a powerful influence on our lives since junior high school. Achievement motivation has been around since McClellan coined the term in the 1950s. But overachievement can be just as debilitating as underachievement.

Helpful Hints:

1. Pick out the overachievers in your own work setting and gauge their overall influence in your own work group.
2. Spend ten minutes each work day helping someone with a work assignment and gauge your effectiveness by the number of times people come to you for advice.
3. Look at the project leaders in your company and write down ten adjectives that describe why they are effective leads.

Coaching Entrepreneurs

Entrepreneurs are a strange breed. They are risk-takers, love challenge, like to develop and grow companies, and love working for themselves. Coaching these folks can be a daunting task for the executive coach. I have a couple of rules to guide those brave coaches who desire to enter the arena of entrepreneurial coaching, similar to a "David Letterman" list:

Number 10: If sounds too good to be true, watch out. Entrepreneurs are full of hope and enthusiasm (some would offer another expletive). It's easy to get caught up in the hype as a personal, business coach. Be sure you maintain your distance and don't get sucked into your client's world of wheeling and dealing.

Number 9: Don't match egos. Entrepreneurs are successful because they are bright, articulate and know their product (service) and consumer base. Many don't want a coach at first, but a third-party (investor, family member) may have offered coaching as a way to moderate management style. Remember, coaches are not consultants. You are not trying to compete with your client, but offer a sounding board with powerful questions to slow down your "boy or girl" wonder to reflect more. In Prochaska's model, entrepreneurs find themselves in the action stage and can be coached more in the contemplation stage to avoid impulsive decisions.

Number 8: Don't be an admirer. It's easy to get caught up in the hype and it's gratifying to the coach to be associated with an exciting person who may become an icon someday. Resist the temptation to be a cheerleader. Your client already has enough "yes" folks and does not need your obsequious adulation. Be fair, but tough. Oftentimes your coaching will involve the "hard truth" of telling like it is. This will be unsettling to your client at first, but in the long run you will gain his/her respect.

Number 7: Maintain boundaries. Some entrepreneurs will want to hire you as their "personal assistant" to be available 24/7 for a monthly contracted fee. Be wary of this arrangement, in spite of the financial rewards. Your job as coach is to remain objective and respect all your clients. Coaches also have a personal life and you may find yourself resentful of that three a.m. call because your client wants to be prepped for a meeting in Sydney, Australia, that you knew nothing about.

Number 6: Accept the change of pace: Coaching entrepreneurs occurs at a faster pace than Fortune 500 clients. Decisions are oftentimes made "on the fly" and timing is everything when one is building a business. Last minute changes to a business plan, an important hire, networking with potential investors, all require multi-tasking on the coach's part.

Number 5: Resist the temptation to use a template model of coaching. By this I mean don't have one way of coaching. Because of the pacing and more personal contact with the business owner and CEO, corporate culture is not as important (as it is with larger companies). Oftentimes, entrepreneurs work in an environment without a culture. Forget about traditional executive coaching techniques as applied to Fortune 500 companies and remember that entrepreneurs thrive on exceptions to the rule.

Number 4: Tolerating instability and uncertainty. Emergent businesses begin without a policy and procedure handbook. Compaq Computers was founded by three folks in Houston on a paper napkin in a fast food restaurant in the early 80s. Coaching entrepreneurs is not for the faint-hearted. Think of yourself as an ER Coach, ready to shift gears as new variables and challenges occur to your client.

Number 3: Pay attention to personal insecurities. This is where you earn your money. Denial and repression are major defense mechanisms used by entrepreneurs to avoid catastrophic scenario planning. For many of your clients change is the driving force to avoid boredom, family responsibilities, and fear of failure. Without getting into therapy with your coaching client, make sure their life is well-rounded and introduce a little fun into the equation.

Number 2: Entrepreneurs are human too. This is a corollary of Rule Number 3 and is a reminder that you need not be intimidated by your client. Many entrepreneurs started from nothing and have lost businesses due to poor planning and impulsive decisions. Resist the temptation to be in awe of your client. Remember that everything you do as a coach is "in service to the client."

Number 1: Say no. This is perhaps the most important rule to remember. If you're not cut out for the fast-pace coaching style with entrepreneurs, then refer your potential client to another coach who specializes in small business coaching or business development. You do yourself and your client a disservice if you practice outside your niche and one bad coaching experience will negate prior successes.

I hope I've given you a few pointers for those of you who wish to coach entrepreneurs, many of whom are small-business owners and sole proprietors. Although the work is hard and challenging, the coaching rewards are remarkable. You have the unique opportunity to shadow a business owner who is developing his/her business in real time with more immediate consequences and change. If you are drawn to the faster pace of coaching small business owners and desire a more personal working relationship, then consider coaching entrepreneurs. Remember that as a coach, you are modeling an entrepreneurial model for your clients. Run your coaching business well and you will serve your clients well.

Helpful Hints:

1. Talk to a small business owner to learn about their business, particularly the start-up phase and where you might be helpful in growing their business.
2. Subscribe to Fortune Small Business and Inc. magazines to get a flavor of who you will be coaching.
3. Get involved with the small business committee with your local chamber of commerce. You will gain useful information and begin to network with business owners.

Coaching Entrepreneurs: Perceiving the Need for Change

We will explore those people who are "ahead of the curve." Much of the material today is drawn from personal experience in developing and managing a fledgling home-health care business in 1986. However, the principles are taken from the chapter of the same name by Barry Dym, Stephen Jenks, and Michael Sonduck in *Executive Coaching: Practices & Perspectives*, Davies Black Publishing, 2002. According to Dym et al there are six challenges for entrepreneurs:
- Perceiving the need for change versus denial and isolation
- Moving toward commitment and planning versus indecision and procrastination
- Accepting the pace of change versus doubt and uncertainty
- Tolerating instability and uncertainty versus regressing to old ways
- Working toward resolution versus fragmentation
- Reintroducing entrepreneurialism versus succumbing to bureaucratic lethargy

Perceiving the need for change: Back in 1986 home health care for the developmentally disabled was taking a back seat to institutional care. In the few instances where community-based services were provided, these services were state-run to provide the stability for parents that there loved ones would be taken care of without risk of bankruptcy or dumping clients on the streets—a fear that was promoted by the public sector to insure continued state funding for bureaucratic, inefficient, and unaccountable services that were sorely lacking initiatives or the latest technology. My partner, Dr. Jon Hannum and I began a privately run group home business for persons who might benefit from long-term care in a less restrictive setting. The state of Texas was in the midst of a class action suit that required downsizing of state schools for persons with mental retardation and "outsourcing and privatization" became buzzwords for offering an alternative business model for providing services. We were able to secure two state contracts in Texas and North Carolina to run six-bed group homes. We were responsible for the strategic plan, business plan, securing a line of credit against pledged receivables (which banks were unwilling to do in 1986 because of the short-term nature of federal funding), hiring and managing staff, and insuring quality services—a small feat for two idealistic former state employees who cashed in their state retirement to form Texas Community Living Ventures. We grew from a staff of two (the principal owners) to 160 in just two years and from one location to 18 locations in two states serving 108 clients and managing two workshops. Needless to say we had no roadmap on how to do this and convincing parents to place their child with us was no easy task. After the first group home was opened in October, 1986, in Houston, Texas, and the first six clients were placed a parent came up to me after a visit with his daughter and said "I'm glad she is here with you; I want you to make a profit because if you don't you'll go out of business and my daughter will have to return to a state school." I was overwhelmed with his comment. He was business savvy and knew that sound management would prove crucial to maintaining longevity for his daughter.

The first two years were start-up. I busied myself with our attorney, insurance rep, housing rentals, community civic organizations, and various other local entities in Houston as we began the push towards privatization. We were an oddity in 1986. People didn't know quite what to think of us: Were we a public entity masquerading as a private enterprise? Were we greedy business types without compassion or training in the field? Were we going to crash and burn? Believe me; I was introduced to scenario thinking immediately. Many a night I spent my four-hour shift worrying about anything and everything that could go wrong. We didn't turn a profit until the fifth month. Jon and I were excited when we finally wrote ourselves a mere $3,000 salary each after five months of working pro bono. The isolation and denial that Dym et al talk about in their chapter about entrepreneurs is very real. One day we were perceived as "trailblazers" who had all the expertise and knowledge. Other days, I scratched my head wondering if we could continue to expand without jeopardizing financial economies of scale and quality services for our clients. It was very lonely those two years for two men in their thirties who knew what to do, but required the backing of a very understanding banker and local communities who believed in what we were doing. Only one community out of 18 ever took us to court over infringement of deed restrictions (there is no zoning in Houston but deed restrictions dictate local housing use). We won at both the local and state court level on the definition of "family" being expanded beyond blood relatives to allow for housing and care in single-family residential neighborhoods. These were upper-middle class neighborhoods with houses priced in the low 100s back in 1986. The typical floor plan was 2400 square feet with four bedrooms (the master for the live-in house parents) to accommodate six clients. More about the programming later, but our business plan was very successful, and we proved that we could provide better services with at the current cost per bed-day being offered in institutional settings.

Helpful Hints:

1. Write a strategic plan that using the SWOT (Strength, Weakness, Opportunities, and Threats) analysis to examine if you can segment your current service or product into a smaller niche that might produce a better result at the same or increased profit margin.
2. Look around your office and list at least ten areas of redundancy and inefficiency.
3. Talk to a private banker or business loan officer about the types of businesses receiving loans now and what makes these business ventures less vulnerable to failure or delinquency in defaulting on their loan.

Coaching Entrepreneurs: Moving Towards Planning and Commitment

This chapter focuses on the second challenge of moving toward planning and commitment in the face of indecision and procrastination. Last chapter we talked about perceiving the need for change which calls for a perceived market demand and funding for your business. Much of the work was drawn from my personal experience of starting a home-health business in 1986. This month we will continue our series with the importance of planning.

How many times have you heard yourself or others day "I wish I had thought of that?" You pick up your garbage bag with built-in ties that eliminate the need and aggravation of your kitchen garbage falling to the newly scrubbed tile floor. Or you take your car in for a tune up and receive a loaner car for the day. Or that pencil you just bought looks just like a number two pencil but the lead automatically advances eliminating the need for a pencil sharpener (I'm not talking about mechanical pencils). Yes, products and services are born everyday. In a recent issue of Fortune magazine, Steve Jobs' commencement address this past May to Stanford graduates resonates around water coolers even today, in an era when commencement addresses are politically correct and sanitized and forgotten immediately. Jobs had three points to deliver to his audience: (1) connect the dots; (2) stay hungry; and (3) stay foolish. His admonition to this year's grads was that "your time is limited, so don't waste it living someone else's life." (Jobs, Fortune, 9/5/05).

Leaders often languish in indecision and uncertainty failing to commit time and resources to a fledging business or idea. I had a friend some years ago who bought a Maaco franchise after losing his job with a major software manufacturer, only to discover that the books were "cooked" by the previous owner and he spent the next two years of his life working 80-hour weeks because he failed to perform the "due diligence" necessary to evaluate the profitability of the business he had bought. Too often, we are lulled into a false sense of security that "hard work and luck" will win the day and make us successful. We've all heard the same success stories: starting a KFC conglomerate at age 76, a fledging open-source web browser (Fire Fox) that now rivals Microsoft, a softer cookie that is packaged to last longer and micro waved to taste just like grandma's tollhouse cookies.

The major mistake entrepreneurs make is that they delegate the planning to others. Entrepreneurs by their very nature are impulsive—they do not plan well. They are concrete random thinkers and they envision results—e.g. what the product or service will look like. Like Steve Jobs said in his commencement address, entrepreneurs have no idea "how to connect the dots." The planning dimension is more than an academic exercise; it is necessary for securing a line of credit, selling your idea to private investors, or creating new markets to fund your enterprise. Many small businesses begin in someone's garage on hopes, dreams, credit card debt, and family loans. This is like offering your manuscript for your mom to read as to its suitability for publication.

Before your business plan is developed one must develop a strategic plan: vision statement, mission statement, and most importantly how to connect the dots using an action plan. Entrepreneurs are keen on staying hungry and foolish but they lack the persistence and due diligence in bringing ideas into products and services. And why not? Entrepreneurs are visionaries by their very nature. They are more likely to be abstract random thinkers where they envision products and services without constraints, timeframes, quality control, delivery times, and product consistency. That's why KFC's "seven secret ingredients" will remain its brand. It's easier to make a sauce than to sell it; look at the thousands of would-be food mavens who are labeling their jars in their garage only to find deaf ears for shelf space at their neighborhood grocery chain. What's missing with this picture? An excellent idea, perhaps, but without a plan to place the product on the shelf or in the catalogue or a delivery system that relies on inflated inventory costs rather than "just in time" inventory perfected by Dell Computers.

So I would add a fourth dimension to Jobs Commencement Address to the 2005 Stanford graduates (remember Jobs never graduated from College; he spent six months at Reed College before dropping out). Besides connecting the dots, staying foolish and hungry, I would execute a plan—remember George Peppard's infamous remarks in the weekly TV series of the 80s—"the A-Team?" I'll never forget it—"I love it when a plan comes together."

Helpful Hints:

1. What are the personality correlates of an entrepreneur? Can you learn creativity from a business school that has an elective in entrepreneurism?
2. Risk-taking behavior: Can it help or hurt when starting a business? How?
3. How many good ideas are never acted upon? Read the book, *Flash of Genius,* by Robert Thornton, for a glimpse of how inventions differ from starting a business.

Reintroducing Entrepreneurialism

The last part of our series in coaching entrepreneurs is reintroducing entrepreneurialism. In past chapters we have covered: perceiving the need for change versus denial and isolation; moving toward commitment and planning versus indecision and procrastination; accepting the pace of change versus doubt and uncertainty, and working towards resolution versus fragmentation.

After introducing change organizations quickly attempt to move their "baby" from R&D to operations for purposes of efficiency and order. If the change is incorporated too quickly managers do not fully comprehend the reasons for the change and "go through the motions" in implementing the change as standard SOP (standard operating procedures). The important person to lead your change team should possess leadership skills rather than managerial skills. Enthusiasm and optimism is the order of the day and new products and services should be rolled out in a stepwise fashion at trade shows and critical consumer demand periods during the year. The movie industry is expert at packaging and marketing a new movie. Have you noticed that the blockbusters suddenly appear twice a year: around July 4th and the holiday season of November and December. The movie most likely sat in a can ready for distribution six months prior to the marketing campaign. Producers understand the movie-going public and that they have more money to spend during mid-summer (after income tax payments to Uncle Sam) and during the holidays. You've experienced this; you're sitting in a movie theatre in August waiting for the main features and you are forced to sit through previews of movies "coming next spring, summer, and fall." The emphasis here is to build demand where none exists. The movie industry has been losing patrons to DVDs and cable TV plus the fact that one cannot possibly produce one winner after another.

Organizations would do well to follow Hollywood in this one respect (I wouldn't carry the comparison too far, however) and that is creating consumer demand for your product or service. Focus groups are important, planning, pacing, and integration *within* the company are all important ingredients in reinventing entrepreneurialism. Do not create management systems *before* your managers have an opportunity to exercise their skills and sell the change within your company by supplying vision and support from a charismatic leader.

Techniques to use in creating innovation include: "Blue Sky" sessions where team members visualize and brainstorm new ideas without critique or competitiveness. MentorCoach, LLC, offers an excellent Blue Sky course taught my Dr. Ben Dean, the founder of MentorCoach which encourages thinking outside the box. Innovation House, LLC, partnered by Dr. Randi Smith is another think tank that offers innovation and leadership skills to executives. You can reach either principal at ben@mentorcoach.com or randis8@earthlink.net.

In conclusion, sometimes change is forced on organizations to remain competitive; but your successful organizations (e.g. Dell) look for opportunities for change as evidenced by their bold move to supply printers and compete with HP for market share. Not every change or new product will be a winner. We will await the results of the **XBOX360** to see if the buying public this past holiday season will remain intrigued with the power and breathe of this interactive video display. Preliminary reports were disappointing in that some products were delivered with "glitches" and the pricing is too high at $400, but the buying public will determine if this new upgrade is successful. **Play Station 3** is due in 2006 and **Nintendo Revolution** is due soon to offer consumers more choices. Service and games inventories will ultimately determine the winner in this battle for Generation XY.

Helpful Hints:

1. Notice how many "sales" retail stores have in a year and the number of people in the stores versus those at the cash registers.

2. The past holiday season what were the big ticket items: look at pricing, marketing, packaging, and store displays. Again notice how many folks were buying electronics, especially IPODs, plasma TVs, digital cameras.
3. Introduce a change within your own company that promotes enthusiasm without the immediate demand for accountability and profit. Employ a process group coach to lead your teams in a Blue Sky brainstorming session.

Personality or Cognitive Learning Style?

One of the biggest challenges of running high performance teams is to blend the different talents of individuals. The astute manager must recognize and take into account differing cognitive learning styles to maximize creativity and performance. The most common reason given for poor team performance is a "clash of personality differences." We've all heard the expression that "too many cooks in the kitchen spoil the stew." Likewise, too many egos in the room spoil the outcome. Instead of focusing on personalities which are difficult to change anyway, Anthony Gregorc (1979) has come up with four different cognitive learning styles that are essential to any team effort. A brief summary of each follows:

Cognitive Sequential: You've seen this type—the geek, drone, and worker bee with nose to the grindstone. The most common characteristic is a sequential thought pattern that relies on a linear progression through a series of calculus: A leads to B to C . . . and finally Z. This is the person who calls a point of order at your local civic association meeting; or the accountant who tells you that you don't have enough revenue to achieve your objectives; or the computer programmer who thinks in code and can't understand why he's on a team in the first place. These folks tend to think in binary terms—i.e. black vs. white, good vs. bad, positive vs. negative. Unless your team leader can hold these folks in check, they will slow down the team with a constant barrage of inconsequential questions that overlook process by focusing too much on procedure. These folks prefer hands-on activities, step by step instructions, and real life examples.

Cognitive Random: This is your team leader who knows what the end result might look like, but does not have the patience to implement a linear procedure to achieve the result. This person already knows that A leads to Z; he or she does not care about details; in fact, details just slow the process down. Their main contribution to team performance is to understand the "big picture" and direct the others towards a consensual goal. Unless your team leader can hold these folks in check they will constantly get the team off course by chasing rabbit holes and keeping the team off task. These learners rarely accept anything on outside authority. They are implementers of change and tend to be impulsive. They don't like to read directions or follow instructions. Instructional methods include independent study, computer games and simulations, multimedia, and playing with software.

Abstract Sequential: These folks tend to think in a logical, linear fashion but with an understanding that knowledge is power. They like solitude, prefer well-organized material, and are highly skeptical. They have trouble picking up subtle nonverbal cues and dislike distractions. They will accept change only after much deliberation. They like written, verbal, and visual instruction. Instructional methods include: lectures, reading, outlines, conducting Internet searches, email, listservs, and audiotapes. Abstract sequential learners may enjoy searching the Internet for information as well as asynchronous communication because they have time to think about their responses.

Abstract Random: These folks are your R&D folks who are futurists and think in the clouds. They are inventors, trailblazers, with a list of patents, trademarks, and copyrights. These learners like to focus on relationships and their emotions. They respond to visual methods of instruction, group discussion, and time for reflection. They may be uncomfortable with distance education because it does not include the emotional involvement of meeting face to face, unless the instructor is careful to build rapport as part of the learning experience. They enjoy evaluating personal experiences. Instructional methods include: video clips, group discussion, videoconferencing, television, case studies, chatrooms, and guest speakers.

So what is the team leader to do with these four types? First, he/she must recognize that all four learning types are essential to "brainstorming" and bringing a new concept to product design and operations. The team's effectiveness is dependent on blending the talents and skills of all four cognitive topologies. Team leaders generally possess at least three of the four learning types and can easily shift from one style to another depending on the developmental stage that the team is working through at the time. In the early stages the "abstract random" types should be permitted to envision the product and allow the "abstract sequential" folks to bring structure to the concepts presented; the "concrete random" team members should keep the group on task, mindful of the group process and allowing all views to be shared. Finally, the "concrete sequential" types should flesh out ideas with timeframes, cost benefit analyses, and quality controls.

A Case Study: When Bill Gates of Microsoft envisioned an interactive game that combined video, audio, and tactile sensory experiences in a 3-D format, he sent his best four "abstract random" thinkers to an alternate campus devoid of distractions. They were given an unlimited budget to come up with a game that would place the gamer *in* the game—the result being the Xbox 360 that took four years to develop. Once the first prototype was completed, the "abstract sequential" thinkers tested the device under different gaming scenarios for compatibility, speed of play, utility, and reality. Next, the "concrete sequential" thinkers wrote the programming code to achieve the necessary steps to bring the prototype to production. Gates himself, while a visionary, supported the Xbox 360 team's efforts by using a "concrete random" approach to keep the team on task with a projected calculus of what he wanted the end user to experience with this new interactive gaming device.

Helpful Hints:

1. At your next team meeting pick out the four different cognitive learning approaches from the questions asked. Which type is the team leader and how is the process affected?
2. Look at GM's concept muscle cars and follow the progression from design to production. How much consumer input

do you see in the final model compared to the prototypes presented?
3. Interview a small business owner and see what his/her dominant cognitive style is and how this affects the profitability of the business.

Gregorc Learning Styles

In this chapter we will introduce you to the talents and cognitive learning styles proposed by Anthony Gregorc in 1984 and how his nomenclature applies to manager and leadership characteristics. First, a primary introduction (the reference website for Gregorc's model is http://www.gregorc.com/gregorc.html). Gregorc proposed a 2 x 2 table with concrete vs. abstract and sequential vs. random, yielding four learning styles: (1) concrete sequential, (2) concrete random, (3) abstract sequential, and (4) abstract random. Let's look at each of these briefly:

Concrete Sequential's Talents:

- Relate sensually with the physical world
- Assess fine degrees of material quality using their physical senses
- Remember specifics
- Street smarts
- Thinks in binary terms—e.g. black/white, good/bad, useful/useless, right/wrong
- Perform duties with exactness in step by step order
- Create practical and useful products to improve the quality of life

Concrete Random's Talents:

- Penetrate complex situations to identify core ideas, principles, motives, and problems

- Use intuition to protect themselves and others from hostile forces and conditions
- Develop non-conventional methods and techniques
- Act independently of others' thoughts, words, and deeds
- Offer charismatic leadership
- Promote social evolution by "pushing the envelope"
- Inspire, teach, guard and protect others

Abstract Sequential's Talents:

- Interact with ideals, values, theories, concepts, models, and paradigms
- Put thoughts into words for others to consider and build upon
- Identify cause/effect relationships via reasoning powers
- Extract themes and key points from mixed or disparate data
- Correlate, analyze, and evaluate information
- Transcend details to grasp the "big picture"
- Be a "voice of reason" and historian for the community

Abstract Random's Talents:

- Attune to their environments and "think with their hearts"
- Relate and nourish the emotional needs of others
- Gather knowledge through images, voice tone, symbols, colors, music, words
- Think holistically
- Cooperate with wide ranges and types of people
- Deal with multiple issues and stimuli simultaneously
- Use their imaginations to create products
- Be a "voice of conscience" for the community

Now let's see how each of the above styles applies to Team Member Characteristics

Concrete Sequential: Dominant members approach teaming:

- Carefully with templates of expectations and standards
- Conservatively in order to assess motives and competencies of others
- Slowly, methodically, and systematically to establish a foundation of trust

Concrete Random: Dominant members approach teaming:

- Assertively, enthusiastically and competitively
- Sociably with minimum concern for social protocol
- Confidently willing to lead if progress doesn't occur

Abstract Sequential: Dominant members approach teaming:

- Intellectually for a meeting of minds
- Politely, impersonally and socially for exchange of thoughts, ideas and opinions
- Carefully with concerns about being tied down by mundane matters

Abstract Random: Dominant member approach teaming:

- Openly with an urge to merge and be a part of something bigger than themselves
- Naturally dedicated to community building
- Comfortably with a desire to nurture, protect and help others

Gregorc Leadership Characteristics:

- Concrete Sequential leaders seek results via the vision becoming reality in everyday life

- Concrete Random leaders seek results with clarity of vision, mind, and spirit safety
- Abstract Sequential leaders seek results with the marriage of theory and practice for organizational action
- Abstract Random leaders seek results with a shared vision within a caring, cooperative, and dynamic community

Helpful Hints:

1. At your next business meeting, look for the different leadership styles: concrete sequential, concrete random, abstract sequential, abstract random. What is the interaction among the members and is it productive?
2. Go to Anthony Gregorc's website and take his Style Delineator profile to see what your dominant and sub-dominant learning styles are.
3. Begin to think of cognitive learning styles rather than personality differences as explanations for miscommunication and assessing teamwork productivity.

Emotional Competence

Our framework for emotional competence is taken from: *Mosaic Competencies for Professional and Administrative Occupations* (U.S. Office of Personnel Management), *Competence at Work* by Spencer and Spencer, and top performance and leadership competence studies published in Richard H. Rosier (Ed.), The *Competency Model Handbook*, Volumes I and II, Boston: Linkage Press, 1994 and 1995. We will talk about self-motivation and social awareness in learning how to work more effectively with our fellow employees.

Self-Motivation: Striving to improve or meet a standard of excellence. People with this competence:
- Are results-oriented, with a high drive to meet their objectives and standards
- Set challenging goals and take calculated risks
- Pursue information to reduce uncertainty and find ways to do better
- Learn how to improve their performance

Commitment: Aligning with the goals of the group or organization. People with this competence:
- Readily make personal or group sacrifices to meet a larger organizational goal
- Find a sense of purpose in the larger mission
- Use the group's core values in making decisions and clarifying choices
- Actively seek out opportunities to fulfill the group's mission

Initiative: Readiness to act on opportunities. People with this competence:
- Are ready to seize opportunities

- Pursue goals beyond what's required or expected of them
- Cut through red tape and bend the rules when necessary to get the job done
- Mobilize others through unusual, enterprising efforts

Optimism: Persistence in pursuing goals despite obstacles and setbacks. People with his competence:
- Persist in seeking goals despite obstacles and setbacks
- Operate from hope of success rather than fear of failure
- See setbacks as due to manageable circumstance rather than a personal flaw

The last area of social competence includes **social awareness** which includes empathy and service orientation.

Empathy: Sensing others' feelings and perspective, and taking an active interest in their concerns. People with this competence:
- Are attentive to emotional cues and listen well
- Show sensitivity and understand others' perspectives
- Help out based on understanding other people's needs and feelings

Service Orientation: Anticipating, recognizing, and meeting customers' needs. People with this competence:

- Understand customers' needs and match them to services or products
- Seek ways to increase customers' satisfaction and loyalty
- Gladly offer appropriate assistance
- Grasp a customer's perspective, acting as a trusted advisor

Helpful Hints:

1. Walk through your neighborhood Wal-Mart and see why customer satisfaction remains priority one with an eye for service orientation.

2. Before you plan this year's resolutions take a moment to see how committed you are to personal sacrifice and if your resolutions resonate with a core value.
3. Many inspirational books have been written in "searching for excellence," beginning with Tom Peter's bestseller, *In Search of Excellence.* Notice the similarities in these "how to" books that emphasize challenging your goals and taking calculated risks. Thinking "outside the box" literally means taking a third dimensional view of your world.

CMO: What is It?

It's inevitable that another "C" appears in the corporate lexicon. First we had the Chief Executive Officer (CEO), then the Chief Operating Officer (COO), the information age ushered in the Chief Information Officer (CIO); now the Director of Marketing receives a big pay hike and his or her own Chieftain title: Chief Marketing Officer (CMO). But is marketing that important in corporate America today? In the August, 2006, *Fortune*, Michael Linton, of *Best Buy*, makes the point that in a shrinking economy, advertising sets apart the winners and losers. "The job of CMO has become one of the highest stressed, shortest-tenured positions in American industry." The average tenure of a CMO is only 23 months. So what makes this job so brutal?

Why don't you ask Bill Gates or Michael Dell if advertising is important? We are inundated with advertising from movies, TV, print media, billboards, radio, and the Internet. Why are sound bites so critical to the buying public? There are many reasons but I wish to posit a few:

1. CMO as psychologist. We are more easily distracted with more information that becomes just background "white noise" to the average consumer. We use the bathroom during commercials; we mute obnoxious sales slogans; we wince at sex and youth selling everything from tanning products to metal buildings. Now that TIVO allows us to bypass commercials when we're taping our favorite TV weekly program, very few commercials even reach us. Despite cable TV and the plethora of "infomercial" channels, we still surf right past the next, greatest kitchen gadget to our favorite ballgame or movie.

2. **CMO as scientist**. Instead of using demographics to define our typical consumer we now rely on high-powered statistical models to predict what a certain consumer will purchase. "One size fits all" no longer suffices for most companies. Direct marketing has failed miserably and is the biggest expense maelstrom on most company balance sheets. The savvy CMO today leverages services and products with other industries. Take the Disney movie, *Cars*, which was a summer blockbuster for Pixar (see earlier blog on John Lasseter) had already positioned a line of products with *McDonalds*, clothing stores, *Toys R Us*, and other "downstream" companies before the movie hit the big screen. Instead of "segmental" marketing, "incremental" marketing is the new buzzword. *Pirates of the Caribbean* is another example of increasing market share over time. More than six hours of film were shot—enough to make two movies which in fact is what the producer and distributor did. If you're going to rent an island and tie up actors for a movie that one knows will work into a sequel, it makes good sense to split the movie and make two movies for the price of one.

3. **CMO as innovator**. Gone are the days of limited shelf life with the advent of the computer and Internet. Despite piracy laws and copyright infringements, marketing is now using the computer as the primary platform for advertising as evidenced by the phenomenal success of Google and Yahoo. People now "pay per click" to shift potential customers to their websites without the obnoxious banners and pop-ups which many spam programs now delete. Welcome advertising to the computer age. Gone is the "man in the grey flannel suit," carrying a briefcase of fliers, mail outs, pens, coffee mugs, and every known ceramic gimmick since snake oil.

4. **CMO as branding agent**. Branding is "corporate speak" for creating customer awareness and demand. If you want to sell cars, you need to understand the psychology behind the market place. You're not going to sell 60k roadsters to "soccer moms." But you can bet that an "empty nester" or

"middle-age crazy" will be in the showroom if you throw in the sun tan lotion, hair transplant, and sunglasses for free.
5. **CMO as service manager**. Marketing and operations use to office in different buildings. Now the two departments act as one knowing that customer loyalty is developed *after* the sale. Dell computer set the model for customer service by offering service contracts tailored to the specific needs of their customers. A computer geek may not need the 3-year in-home service package, but the busy college student without his/her own IT department and little cash after the sale wants their computer fixed before an eight a.m. paper is due tomorrow.
6. **CMO as futurist**. Ad campaigns use to rely on time-limited slogans. Remember the "hungry man" soups? The demographics have changed to a fitness fanatic culture that relies more on carb and calorie counts than portion size. Trending is another tool in the CMO's arsenal to remain competitive despite changing times. We know that the "Boomer" is the largest buying public today with the most discretionary income. Products designed for the Gen Xers and Yers should resonate equally with Boomers who are near retirement in five years. Witness the growth of adult living programs marketed under various names from "retirement community" to "memory center."
7. **CMO as consumer**. It takes more than just believing in your service or product. It requires customer loyalty. It makes no sense for Toyota plant employees to fill up the parking lot with Ford 150 pickups. Nor does it make sense for Hollywood types to have *Dell* computers when *Apple* has the exclusive contract with movie moguls.
8. **CMO as process manager**. "Connectivity" is the name of the game for marketing today and no one does this better than Steve Jobs of *Apple*. The IPOD has been a tremendous success with the *iTunes* free software and connecting with *Verizon* is a great way to offer music and video to "entertainment junkies" who get adrenaline rushes with the next IM, video

stream, or picture of their favorite movie star. By connecting with other companies and products companies can extend the half-life of their products and services.
9. **CMO as virtual assistant.** Everyone knows the success of "Geek Squad" complete with lavender VW beetles. Instead of being placed on hold by someone who barely speaks English five time zones away from you, a *real* person comes to your work or residence to fix your hardware or software problems. Good service sells; bad service destroys customer loyalty.
10. **CMO as change agent.** Today's CMO must work closely with R&D to develop the next "mousetrap" that everyone will want. Witness the phenomenal success of Microsoft's Xbox 360. Bill Gates had the foresight to give four budding entrepreneurs their own campus and building for four years with an unlimited budget to develop the next generation of gaming, knowing that interactive gaming would be the next wave with websites, marketing, and hardware servers all contributing to "real time" competitive gaming.

Helpful Hints:

1. Go into a Best Buy store and notice that "geek squads" are available for those Techophobic Newbies who can't turn the on/off switch.
2. Go into a Target store and notice that the aisles are wider with less clutter and more colorful signs to direct the consumer.
3. Go into an HEB grocery store and notice that one must first pass through the produce department to get to the meat and canned goods sections; also notice there are no shortcuts to the cash register, guaranteeing that the impulse shopper will pick up a few extra items along the way to check-out.

Crazy Bosses

Fortune's current June issue has an entertaining and humorous book excerpt by Stanley Bing's *Crazy Bosses,* Harper Collins, 2007. Many of us have worked for these folks in the past (some of us are unfortunate enough to still be working for these bosses). The archetypes are summarized below:

The Bully:

Bill O'Reilly epitomizes this boss who "takes no prisoners' when barking orders to the troops. He or she relies on innuendo, fear, and threats to motivate their staff. Things one can do to combat the aggressive and insensitive boss are: provide operating assistance, play hard to get will make the bully respect you, stay out of striking distance, use common sense and make yourself scarce during the "shrapnel meetings."

The Paranoid:

Richard III epitomizes this boss who shuts his door refers all calls and visitors to you, and doesn't come out of his office. He may even have a secret, panic exit, to escape would-be staffers seeking advice. Actions one can take to deal with the paranoid boss include: be a little edgy yourself, honor the closed door and do your own thing, don't beat yourself up, remain effective and productive to maintain your sanity.

The Narcissist:

Liberace is the epitome of the narcissist. He views all around him as tiny flecks in the fantasy spectacle of life. Deadlines are blown, opportunities delayed, while your boss is busy getting a $400 haircut for his quarterly TV broadcast to the troops. Sound bites, flashy videos, make-up artist, a contingent of celebrities are important to the narcissist.

To combat the narcissist, one should: maintain his/her comfort, remain highly effective, keep your boss's show on the road, build his insecurities, and find his hot button to maintain a sense of control that "you will handle everything for him."

The Wimp:

FEMA's former director Mike Brown epitomizes the wimp who is obsessed with bureaucracy and process. A one-time boss of the author criticized employees who did not fill in the bullets that were used to itemize notes on memos. Actions one can take to deal with the wimp include: cover your butt as you cover his, remember you're protected (he won't fire you), remain solid and consistent to cover up his lack of purpose and resolve.

The Disaster Hunter:

George W. Bush is a disaster hunter who looks for crises to maintain a sense of control as commander in chief. Another candidate for Disaster Hunter is Alexander Haig (I'm in control here) after Nixon's departure. Bill Clinton was another explosion waiting to happen with his self-destructive power (remember Monica?). Politicians prefer to keep the pot stirred to keep the limelight on them as "in the saddle." Stanley Bing is not kind to our 43rd President who is described as a morphed wimp, paranoid, narcissist, bully, and disaster hunter. (count Dick Cheney as well). Actions one can take if you work for this kind of boss include: get tough, be organized, don't look back, and stay busy without concerning yourself with effectiveness or productivity.

Helpful Hints:

1. Which description fits your current boss and what actions do you take to get along? Are you effective in dealing with his/her eccentricities?
2. What is your own management style? Ask a coach to evaluate your personality and managerial approach by asking the troops anonymously how you manage during crises and the doldrums.
3. Read Daniel Goleman's book on *Emotional Intelligence* to help you become a more effective manager of people.

Section Three: Career Coaching

Section Three deals with career coaching for those individuals who want to change careers. For some, they want to start their own business; for others, they want off the corporate track realizing they have hit the "glass ceiling" and they wish to spend their energies following an earlier passion. Regardless of the reason, career coaching is about rekindling the passion and excitement of work and giving folks realistic expectations and hope about how to execute their dream plan. The chapters to follow deal with: where are you headed, signature strengths, putting your strengths to work, core values, emotional competence, searching for your dream job, looking for the next job, retirement issues, career coaching for job change, and baby boomers starting a second career.

Where Are You Headed? The Career Change Coach

Life coaching has been around longer than executive coaching in the coaching community. A listing of specialties within the International Coach Federation (ICF) lists more "life coaches" than any other category. Another category of coaching focuses on "career development and change." With many mergers and acquisitions as corporations aspire to "take a larger piece of the action" executives are left without jobs and no place to go. Unless they have another interest that can be parlayed into an income stream, these fine seasoned warriors are left clueless and immobile, physically and emotionally.

A ripe area for coaching and one that I've had a modicum of success with is "Career Change" coaching that takes a holistic view of the person, especially their strengths and limitations, goals, desires, ambition, cognitive learning style, and personality.

A typical opening "pitch" to potential coaching clients might be: Do you find yourself at a crossroad in your life? Are you overwhelmed with career choices and information from employers, career sites, outplacement, job counselors, websites such as *CareerBuilder* and *Monster* who have a multitude of positions with excessive criteria and meager pay? Would you like someone in your corner who can objectively match your interest, skills, and personality traits to fit a job where you will feel at home?

Career change coaching (CCC) for displaced executives is intended to insure:
- Goals match aptitude and ability
- Emotional support during your job search
- Work with potential employers

- Personality tests to measure positive interpersonal traits and emotional intelligence
- Value assessments to measure core beliefs
- Identity issues that affect career choices
- Ongoing support after your job offer to insure a productive start and learning curve

What makes for a good CCC coach? A number of traits are important which I shall refer to as the 10 *Es*:

Empathy: Your coach should have the ability to tap into your fears, doubts, and worries about changing careers, especially if you've been in a given job for more than ten years. Preferably, your coach should have at least two different career changes prior to their coaching experience. I'm reminded of the authors of "The Alpha Male Syndrome" where one of the co-authors (Eddie Erlandson) was a cardiovascular surgeon before embarking on a highly successful coaching career.

Educable: Your coach should be a good listener and willing to adapt to new technology and emerging markets. Choose a coach that is well-read, especially in business journals, and a futurist thinker that asks "what is possible?"

Empowered: Your coach should bring positive energy to your career choices and decisions. This is more than a transfer of power from the coach to the displaced executive; the process is derived from a "co-active" coaching relationship that is built on trust, commitment, and integrity. The strength of the relationship with your coach will determine success, not the coach's qualifications or the client's desire to be coached.

Encouraging: Displaced executives don't need to "cry over spilt milk." Instead they need positive encouragement and motivation that elicits hope and enthusiasm. In some sense your coach is a "cheerleader" who stands in your corner, pushing you to accept challenges that you once thought impossible or improbable.

Enlightened: Career choices and decisions are not made with a heuristic methodology. Intuition is imperative if a coach is to offer insight into their clients' dreams, desires, and ambitions. After all the tests and scores are reviewed a job offer and acceptance of same boils down to a "gut feeling" that "this is the job for me." This is not a mystical or elusive quality but an intuitive "hit" that taps unrealized energy in the job applicant.

Ernest: You want a coach who is determined to work for you in helping you to realize and support potential for change. Unemployed executives are not "happy campers." After years of a steady income stream, the realization that financial obligations continue despite a drastic drop in revenue calls for a coach who understands the seriousness of your situation and has experienced the same in his or her own life. Nothing motivates like being in the trenches with your client. All the coaching books in the world will not lend credibility to your coach unless they have experienced limited income and financial risks themselves.

Eventful: Unemployed executives are not a happy lot. Worry, doubts, and fears pervade the initial shock of no job. In the near-term, these feelings are necessary to promote change, however painful. A successful career transition builds on a series of decisions over time, marked by critical and notable events that signal change as a process from uncertainty to certainty.

Exceptional: If you are between jobs you don't want to invest in a coach right out of school with little or no "real world" business experience. Academic consultants are ill equipped to provide the knowledge, skills, and experience necessary for a successful career transition. Talk is cheap; ask your prospective coach for their resume. Any respectable coach will gladly comply. Also ask for list of past coaching clients (with their permission of course) and ask them how the coach assisted them in a successful career move.

Exemplary: Any coach who is coaching others on career changes should lead by example. You want a coach who has made at least two major career moves across two different industries. A coach familiar with start-ups, small business coaching, mergers and acquisitions is preferable to a coach who has only "counseled" individuals without considering the context and industry requirements and standards for chosen professions.

Extroverted: My bias is that a successful career coach should be an extrovert. You want a coach who is skilled politically and socially—someone who has mastered organizational culture, knows small business, networks with other coaches, belongs to the ICF, adept at forging and renewing business relationships, and belongs to organizations like a local chamber or other professional organizations.

In this chapter, I've given you ten criteria for selecting a career change coach who will increase your chances of landing another job in the same industry or can offer a glimpse into a new career opportunity where fantasy and reality merge to create what is possible, given your intellectual, emotional, and personal qualities. It's much harder to seek re-employment alone. You need a professional coach who exhibits the above qualities—where your success is embraced by your coach—where your opportunities for change are dependent on a strong coaching relationship built on trust and integrity. Good luck in your next career!

Helpful Hints:

1. Next time you ask for a coach, ask for them to email their resume to you. Make sure they have the business experience necessary to understand your current situation.
2. If you're between jobs join a networking group of displaced executives. Many churches offer a job networking group where businesses place ads.
3. Even if you're successfully employed, send your resume anonymously to a job that would be a "next step" for you. Do you receive a reply? Why not?

Signature Strengths

Executive development has moved away from working with KSAs (knowledge, skills, and abilities) in favor of signature strengths. Instead of 360 evaluations that focus on one's weaknesses with a remediation plan, executives are now assessed for their strengths which are less resistant to change, but nevertheless, adaptable to change. The approach is more positive and emphasizes one's talents and how to blend individual talents to the company's mission, goals, strategies, and objectives. One approach is Marty Seligman's VIA Signature Strengths Survey found on his website: www.authentichappiness.com. Another approach is Gallup's Strength Finder assessment found on their website: www.gallup.com. Both approaches are in the developmental stages but open the door for further research and application to individual, group, and corporate environments. For example, suppose John Doe, CEO, is an empathic, warm, caring, and good process person. He has excellent teamwork skills, can bring groups to consensus, and heal open wounds left by competing factions. However, he is also charged with generating additional capital which requires marketing and fundraising skills, which is not one of his signature strengths (perseverance, industriousness, persistence). Instead of replacing John Doe and incurring exorbitant replacements and retraining costs (including buying out his contract and stock options), it might be easier to introduce John to a marketing environment. One approach might be to have the CEO spend a couple of months with his marketing director, purely as an observer and view the KSAs necessary for marketing to consumers. Using John's existing signature strengths, he might "reframe" his marketing strategy as "giving value and service to the customer that is consistent with his core values and beliefs of fairness."

Coaches can play an important role in "shadowing" executives and giving them a sounding board for their thoughts, feelings, and actions. The coach should be mindful of his client's signature strengths and play into his strong suit to help the client achieve results that might lend themselves to less salient strengths. This bolsters self-confidence which is critical to desired results. In this day of uncertainty, mergers, layoffs, and "you're fired" vis a vis Trump's reality show, *The Apprentice*, it is refreshing to know that emotional intelligence and personality traits can be modified somewhat to set the stage for change. The signature strength movement is nothing more than a replay of accentuating the positive (positive reinforcement) as opposed to punishing executives for results beyond their control. Executives, after all, are people too, with the same fears, doubts, and anxiety as the rest of us. I'm reminded of what one executive told me a long time ago: no one ever has 100 percent of the information to make an informed decision, but you do the best job you can, based on the information you have available. Also understand that decisions do not occur in a vacuum, and the process of decision-making occurs along a continuum with no right or wrong answer. In the age of quick fixes, bottom lines, sound bites, ROIs, executive performance still comes down to desire and motivation.

Helpful Hints:

1. Take the VIA survey found on Marty Seligman's website: www.authentichappiness.com. Are there any surprises?
2. List your strengths and how these traits have helped you make good decisions in the past. Do your strengths match past and present job assignments?
3. In your next coaching engagement, focus on your client's strengths to achieve change in his or her life.

Go Put Your Strengths To Work

Marcus Buckingham has written an informative book, *Go Put Your Strengths To Work,* which focuses on the "glass being half full" in each of our talent banks. The author had 17 years of research working with the Gallup Organization before forming his own consulting company. I had the good fortune of hearing a live telecast of Marcus on a worldwide leadership conference in Chicago among other notable speakers such as Jimmy Carter, Colin Powell, Michael Porter, Carly Fiorina, and John Ortberg.

Buckingham makes the valid point that in most Western societies weaknesses are given too much attention in our school, parenting, employee performance which tries to correct our inadequacies so that everyone should be at the same level of skill in all areas. He talks about our personalities being formed by age six as to competitiveness, cooperation, logical thinking, and team-building. What remains in this nature vs. nurture controversy is to build on individual strengths that complement other co-workers rather than everyone being "utility players." In Jack Welch's terms (author of Winning), everyone has the potential to be a "star" player in their chosen skill which should be managed and integrated for the best result.

His definition of strength are those activities that make you feel strong. In his language of SIGN one uses:

Success: those activities that you're successful at

Instinct: Intuitive skills that one is drawn to *before* the activity

Growth: Inquisitiveness that makes one want to practice repeatedly *during* the activity; for others it's being in the Zone, where focus and time intersect

Needs: is how one feels *after* the activity is completed; exhilaration, tiredness, a sense of a job well done

Capture, clarify, and confirm your strengths in the first step in identifying one's strengths. A simple 3x5 will suffice for this exercise. Examples of capturing your strengths include: I am strong when . . .
- I'm coaching my team to meet their quarterly goals
- Collaborating with others to develop content for our new service offerings
- Designing powerful conversations to help people have the impact they intend
- Leading or participating in brainstorming sessions for engineering solutions to problems
- Synthesize and compile information into a clear report

A strengths-based model leads to feelings of: powerful, confident, natural, smooth, on fire, great, authentic, that was easy, awesome, when can I do this again?

A weak-based model leads to feelings of: drained, time's going by slowly, I can't concentrate, frustrated, wiped out, irritated, bored, and forced.

A quick way to look at your strengths and weaknesses is to write down your activities for a week and put them under two columns, labeled: "I loved it or I hated it." The feelings noted above will give you a clue as to whether or not your talents are being used in a tactical and productive way to impact your department, section, team, or other working unit.

A strengths-based approach to skill development is a continuous learning process. If you find yourself in a job that underutilizes your strengths or your boss doesn't know how to work from your strengths there are four strategies before leaving your current position or negotiating a new role for you in the company.
- Identify exactly how and where each strength helps you in your current role
- Find missed opportunities to leverage each strength in your current role
- Learn new skills and techniques to sharpen each strength
- Build your job towards each strength

If one is fortunate to have a boss who is not intimidated by your candor and suggestions for redefining your role, Buckingham advises one to have a "strengths chat" with their boss to capture, clarify, and confirm their greater utility to the team and company.

Implicit in this strength-based model is development of "high performance teams" led by competent and intuitive managers who collectively use individual team members' strengths to achieve a common goal—e.g. innovative product design at lower cost, redefining branding, reducing lead time from product design to implementation. This team-building approach requires the manager to keep a list of each member's top three strengths and how they uniquely contribute to the overall goal of the mission, goal, activity, etc.

The author's concluding affirmation to all of us is three-fold:
- You've always known what your strengths are.
- You've always known what lies within you.
- So trust your strengths, be proud of them, and take your stand.

Helpful Hints:

1. Pick up a copy of Buckingham's book and take the strengths test at www.simplystrengths.com.
2. What are your top three strengths? How often do you get to use these at work? If the answer is less than weekly, you will feel drained and not very useful in your job.
3. What are your top three weaknesses? Does your boss know about these? Are you still trying to "fit in" with your co-workers? What is your boss doing to help you work *around* your weaknesses as opposed to *correcting* or worse yet, *ignoring them.*

Core Values

Much has been written about core values. William Bennett's groundbreaking book, *Book of Virtues*, talks about the absence of "politeness" in the body politic. Bill O'Reilly's cable news program "The O'Reilly Factor" is syndicated internationally. He talks about "factors" that are really core values that have changed since the quiet 1950s (our parents' generation which Tom Brokaw describes as the "The Greatest Generation."). What do individual core values have to do with corporate America, you ask? The short answer is "plenty." One has only to look at the Enron, WorldCom, Fannie Mae scandals to know that greed is alive and well in corporate America. Talk to your neighbor who was laid off because his or her job was "outsourced" to another country to boost profits; talk to those disabled individuals who are still discriminated against in the workplace, in spite of the American Disabilities Act (which does not apply to companies with fewer than 100 employees). Look at our consumer spending and rising individual bankruptcies because we choose to purchase on credit using money we don't have (corporations do the same thing). Look beyond the "mission statement" of large corporations to see who gets promoted, who survives, and who wins. MBA programs may give you one ethics course in their programs, but it's more lip service than trying to infuse ethics into a corporate culture. Despite all the teambuilding efforts to make people work together in the workplace, "individualism" is alive and well because competition remains the group dynamic most admired in corporate America. In contrast, Pacific Rim countries value "consensus" and CEO salaries are not 300 times an entry-level worker's salary.

So what does this all mean to those of us who work to enhance the bottom line for our bosses? Social psychologists in the 40s coined a term called "cognitive dissonance" which simply means: when your beliefs are disparate from group norms, you are either co-opted by the system or you remain dissatisfied in your job. The people whom I coach fall into both categories and call me because they are "stressed out" at work. After looking at their personal goals and doing a balanced life and values clarification exercise, it is apparent why we are stressed out. We simply are not adhering to our core basic beliefs in the workplace and either "work to live" or "live to work" depending on our level of job security.

Another factor influencing our decisions to work for ourselves or others has to do with our "risk-taking" behaviors. My father was a career naval officer and served his country dutifully during WW II, until he retired in 1965. His job assignments (orders) were prepared for him by his superiors and he never questioned his fate—it had been decided for him and he was comfortable with this. He didn't buy his first home until I was 12, because base housing was always provided to him and his family. His jobs were well-defined, structured, and low-risk, while offering great job security. He retired after 23 years and began a second career with a private personnel headhunting firm. Despite a difficult transition to a base salary plus commission, he thrived in his "civilian" job because he was willing to take charge of his life. Those of you who work in federal, state, or county jobs know how important job security and benefits are. I'm not knocking public service. I worked in this environment for eleven years before "striking out on my own." My experience in state government was invaluable but there's a big difference between OPM (other people's money) and MM (my money). I learned this the hard way when applying for corporate hospital jobs after a successful administrative career in state government. My resume was impressive except for one area: P and L (profit and loss). It took two stints at running my own business to convince myself and others that "calculated risk-taking" can pay off if one works smarter and harder. The biggest advantage to working for yourself is that it's easier to merge individual and work values. I enjoy helping others and coaching is a way to blur the lines between work and play.

Helpful Hints:

1. COREMAP is a useful tool to look at individual and organizational values to see how well you fit within the values espoused and practiced by your company.
2. Take out a sheet of paper and make two columns marked "my values" and "company values." What did you discover?
3. Put together a five-year plan for transitioning to a smaller company or working for yourself. You can minimize the financial risk by spending some extra time each week reading and taking small business classes at your local community college.

Emotional Competence

This chapter we are typically thinking about family activities, busy schedules, and trying to adjust to the demands of family and jobs. Mental health types suggest that the holiday season can be the most stressful part of the year. An astute manager who is emotionally competent has a better chance of guiding his (her) team through this stressful period while still focusing on end of the year goals for stockholders and employees. I would like to introduce you to the Emotional Competence Framework from: *Mosaic Competencies for Professional and Administrative Occupations* (U.S. Office of Personnel Management); Spencer and Spencer, *Competence at Work*, and top performance and leadership competence studies published in Richard H. Rosier (ed.), *The Competency Model Handbook*, Volumes I and II, Boston: Linkage Press, 1994 and 1995.

Self-Awareness

Emotional Awareness: This is recognizing one's emotions and their effects. People with this competence:
- Know which emotions they are feeling and why
- Realize the links between their feelings and what they think, do, and say
- Recognize how their feelings affect their performance
- Have a guiding awareness of their values and goals

Accurate self-assessment: Knowing one's strengths and limits. People with this competence are:
- Aware of their strengths and weaknesses
- Reflective, learning from experience

- Open to candid feedback, new perspectives, continuous learning, and self-development
- Able to show a sense of humor and perspective about themselves

Self-confidence: Sureness about one's self-worth and capabilities. People with this competence:
- Present themselves with self-assurance; they have "presence or charisma"
- Can voice unpopular views and do what is right
- Are decisive despite uncertainties and pressures

Self-Regulation

Self-control: Managing disruptive emotions and impulses. People with this competence:
- Manage impulsive and distressing feelings
- Stay composed, positive and reflective in trying moments
- Think clearly and are focused under pressure

Conscientiousness: Taking responsibility for personal performance. People with his competence:
- Meet commitments and keep promises
- Hold themselves accountable for meeting their objectives
- Are organized and careful in their work

Adaptability: Flexibility in handling change. People with this competence:
- Multi-task demands, shifting priorities, and rapid change
- Adapt their responses and tactic to fit fluid circumstances
- Are flexible in how they see events

Innovativeness: Being comfortable with and open to novel ideas and new information. People with this competence:
- Seek out fresh ideas from a wide variety of sources
- Entertain original solutions to problems
- Generate new ideas
- Take fresh perspectives and risks in their thinking

Helpful Hints:

1. Talk to someone this month in your office whom you don't know much about and ask them what they like to do in their free time.
2. Take time from your busy schedule to reflect on how you handle change. Do you foster anxiety and resentment in others or do you bring out the best in them?
3. How creative are you willing to be? Take a risk this month and look into an activity that you've been putting off for a long time.

Still Searching for Dream Job

After months of no interviews are you fast losing hope and have you resigned yourself to keeping your current job? Take my own advice that I give corporate clients and float your resume to see how marketable you are. What I've learned in this process are the following do's and don'ts:

Do's:

1. Be careful to limit your resume to your most recent experiences; if you're over fifty you don't run the risk of dating yourself.
2. Be sure to network with your colleagues; let them know you're in the job market and give them your business card; if necessary, make up new cards stating your objective and why you would be a good fit for jobs you're looking for.
3. Be specific: don't use CEO if you're not willing to specify type of industry. Most industries hire from within and senior management experience in one industry (e.g. hospital administration) does not necessarily transfer to B2B business development.
4. Prepare specific cover letters for each job you're applying for to let recruiters know you've read their job specs and can address each point in the job description.
5. Check on jobs every day if you're using one of the Internet search engines like Monster or CareerBuilder. Specify "last 24 hours" to eliminate redundancies. Many jobs are pulled off the board and placed back on later. Keep a job file of the jobs you've applied for.

6. Be prepared to relocate and pay moving expenses because most senior jobs want to hire locally to eliminate this expense.
7. Remain optimistic in light of the fact that your chances of hitting a senior position over 100k to be quite slim unless you have an "inside edge." Many companies post publicly to meet EEO requirements.
8. Stay away from recruiters who will waste your time with phone interviews; also stay away from marketing and investment schemes.
9. List critical success factors in your resume that relates to "bottom line" results—e.g. emerging new markets, increased market share, cost savings, etc.
10. Use milestones or benchmarks to describe complex job assignments in the past; be specific, measurable, attainable, realistic, and time-limited (SMART).

Don'ts:

1. Don't list dates when you received degrees if you're over fifty.
2. Don't pay recruiters upfront fees to look for you.
3. Don't reply by email unless specifically requested to do so; many emails are deleted immediately and not entered into a job bank and kept for six months if you apply via a menu-driven job board.
4. Don't list references unless specifically requested to do so. This limits your options depending on job you're seeking.
5. Never give out your social security number over the Internet. Call or email the recruiting authority and explain your reasons for security.
6. Don't list job titles on your resume; instead use benchmarks and SMART goals.
7. Don't list any personal information on your resume; this can be used against you; wait for a phone or personal interview.

8. Don't expect a job within six months; the rule of thumb is one month for each 10k increase in salary—e.g. a 100k position typically takes 10 months to fill.
9. Don't be swayed by slick bonuses; stay with base salary and benefits to compare job offers.
10. Don't oversell yourself; you're setting yourself up for a quick exit if you find yourself in a job that you can't handle. After the "honeymoon" you're looking at additional relocation expenses, no job, no contacts, and burned bridges.

In summary, I advise clients to update their resumes and "put yourself out there" to see what skills you need to improve. This gives you a growth plan for future coursework and self-study. This process also humbles you and makes one appreciate your present circumstances and why you've stayed in your current job. Unless you hate your job, you probably already receive adequate compensation and job satisfaction. It's difficult to switch jobs after age fifty. This becomes the glass ceiling in corporate America and unless you're willing to "go it alone" you might stick it out another 12-15 years until retirement. I've learned that if you're basically an entrepreneur and value your time and control over your hours, then working for someone else becomes problematic for both. You will most likely find yourself competing with your CEO for running the company and your "maverick" style will be viewed as counterproductive to "consensus management" and loyalty to the company. There's truth in the adage that people work for themselves because either: no one else would hire them, or they wouldn't work for anyone else.

Helpful Hints:

1. Redo your resume using the above points in this chapter.
2. Ask yourself if you would hire a person with your resume; why not?
3. Get a career change coach to help you with your resume and cover letter.

Looking For Another Job?

About every three years I decide to leave my safe world of private practice therapy and begin a job hunt for a salaried position that complements my coaching practice. I begin with the usual Internet search engines: *Career Builder and Monster*, along with some lesser-known search engines. I've also selected companies (like Johnson and Johnson) and industries (pharmaceutical, hospital, governmental) that I would like to work for and placed a resume and profile on their employment websites.

The next step is to rebuild your resume that accurately reflects your knowledge, skills, and abilities (KSAs) and include an objective statement at the top of your resume. Be sure that the resume is less than three pages, preferably one. Use action verbs that are "results" oriented.

Networking is also important, so be sure to put out the word that you're looking for a new challenge. Don't be afraid to extend yourself with your local Chamber of Commerce and "unsafe" contacts outside your immediate circle of colleagues. I'm looking to use my human relationship skills in any corporate HR department that values their employees as much as their customers. I've applied for senior management positions outside of the healthcare sector, if the KSAs are transferable. Doing executive evaluations and team-building is the same skill that works in most labor-intensive jobs.

Corporate culture is critical to a successful job search. Do you wish to work in a top-down, bureaucratic organization after working for yourself for 15 years or do you prefer a smaller company with entrepreneurial possibilities for a "spin off" company? Look to see if any personal investment is required and stay away from those recruiters who have no jobs but only want to sell you a dream. Many of these scams are "multi-level" marketing ploys designed to take your money and waste your time. Executive recruiters and "headhunters" are okay IF THE HIRING AGENCY is paying their commission. Don't take money out of your pocket when looking for that next job.

Don't limit yourself geographically unless you have heavy family obligations that limit your travel time. I would also recommend that you develop a strategic plan for finding your next job. Include a vision, mission, and goal statements along with a SWOT analysis (strengths, weaknesses, opportunities, and threats) that will assist or limit you in your competing for that next challenge. Remain optimistic, but not overly grandiose. Be confident, but not cocky. And finally, be your authentic self and don't sell an image.

Helpful Hints:

1. Rewrite your resume even if you're not looking for a new job. What do you notice about your past accomplishments and settings, tenure, reasons for leaving?
2. Do a computer search for jobs that fit your qualifications and see what's out there. You may want to stay put and be happy with your salary and job attributes.
3. Write a one-page narrative that sells your qualifications and why another company needs a person with your skills and talents.

Still Looking?

Are you still in this job hunting business with no results; not one interview; only recruiting agencies and multi-level marketing schemes who want to take your money to give you a "leg up" on jobs that are never advertised on job boards or anywhere else—sound familiar? It's like paying for "insider information." Your first call was from a national headhunter who wanted to "invite" you to a closed meeting after reviewing your resume and cover letter. Beware of the word, "invite." If you begin to feel like a fish, then you are correct. You later found out by bypassing the caller that ultimately you would be asked to pay a one-time fee of $11,000 to become part of a national consulting network. Politely say, "no thanks" and ask the VP to remove your name from the "invite" list. My own personal experience was a company in Texas who wanted inside sales staff to buy and sell their assessment tool products to business and industry. Again, I politely refused and thanked the caller for his offer, but reminded him that I didn't want to compete against myself (I don't think he got the hint).

My advice if you insist on using search engines like *careerbuilder.com* and *monster.com* is to not spend more than five hours a week. Set your search agents to select narrowly so that you meet minimum qualifications for jobs you're interested in. Don't waste your time looking for manufacturing jobs if you have no experience. This seems like a "no brainer" but these jobs do come up if you don't narrow your field of industry. For my search, I selected three search agents: CEO, senior management, and consulting in health, government, and business development. I included all 50 states for one and three states for the remaining two search agents. I check daily so I asked to be notified daily and set my search to the "last 24 hours." This way I don't waste time with redundant job advertisements.

Now to the point of applying online versus email. I prefer to apply online because it gives you the opportunity to provide a cover letter with your resume that you can paste into the resume section of your application. Be sure to write cover letters specific to the jobs you are applying for which implies you did a little homework about the company and are not randomly sending out cover letters. There's nothing worse that telling your prospective employer that you have experience working in the public sector if you're applying to a Fortune 500 company. Also be sure to have different versions of your resume depending on type and level of job you're applying to—e.g. don't list entry-level jobs if you're applying for executive positions; typically one goes back to the last four jobs or fifteen years of relevant experience. Be sure not to have lapses in your employment dates because it usually indicates a resignation, termination, or illness.

On a more serious note, I'm finding that job boards are not the way to go for high-level executive positions. Granted I'm aiming high because I'm satisfied with what I'm now doing but I'm interested in the process of looking for another job in another industry and what's available on the Internet. Most companies do respond with an acknowledgement of your application, many of which are driven by computer programs with data-based management. I did to my surprise receive a written acknowledgement by snail mail for one CEO position and that the process would take another two months before interviews were lined up.

There are also basic dos and don'ts to being interviewed by phone and giving too much information is equivalent to talking too much about yourself and indicates to the other person that you're inexperienced or nervous. Better to remain quiet and respond to the questions that are asked than volunteering information.

Helpful Hints:

1. Try a job search on the Internet using a wide range of parameters and see what you get as a response; next narrow your search to three specific cities you might consider

relocating and change your salary to at least 25% more than you're making now.
2. Find a book on job searches at your local bookstore and peruse the information. Understand that professional headhunters only land one job for every ten applicants; and your chances are less than that.
3. Look up a company you'd like to work for on the Internet and go to their home page and look for job listings. Most of your Fortune 500 companies post jobs on the Internet and they offer to keep your resume on file for six months.

Retire Rich?

The current issue of *Fortune's* cover shows a 50-something couple overlooking a serene beach in St. Martin in the French West Indies. You would think that they had made all the right decisions—e.g. maxed 401 (k) contributions, no college expenses with astute pre-tax tuition plans, riding the market with the help of their financial advisor, and a dual income from an entrepreneurial business sold for millions. What, do you think, is the secret to their financial success?

Make no mistake about it. The vignettes presented are from upper middle class families who had connections to great jobs: AMEX Stock Exchange, a chemist turned food packager, mid-level Quest communications manager, corporate public and investor relations, and a retired naval officer after 20 years. These couples both had good jobs, most likely in the top 5%, and successful start-ups made possible from retirement nest eggs, minority business loans, and sheer luck. It looks too good to be true, but do these folks really represent the boomers who are now 62 and approaching retirement?

It's no surprise that another article in the same issue gives retirement lessons by Susan Kaufman, a research associate for *Fortune*.

1. **Don't assume** you'll be spending less money. Most financial investment formulae *underestimate* the amount of money required for retirement because people assume they will continue their pre-retirement standard of living. Even if you're lucky enough to have your house paid off, you should not overlook ways of cutting back: eating out, multiple vacations, leasing new cars every two years, two homes, not banking your adult children, wasting money on life insurance, and subscribing to multi-year (more than

four) long-term care health insurance. The rule of thumb is that one will need 70% of their pre-retirement income to maintain their standard of living.
2. **Free time costs money**. Get a hobby and stay busy to keep from dumping money in extravagant toys. Travel constitutes the largest expense for retirees; the more practical option is to plan early and buy property where you want to retire; instead of retiring in a tourist area (e.g. Sedona, Arizona), you can pick a working class town 30 miles away (Cottonwood).
3. **Consider working in your retirement**. Your brain is the most important commodity you have and your ability to earn an income does not diminish with age. Work will avoid major identity issues with workaholics. The more all consuming your career, the more difficult your retirement without some work outlet.
4. **Make sure you and your spouse are compatible** because you will be spending *a lot* of time together. Couples need to renegotiate their time together and their routines, just as they did early in their marriage, according to Phyllis Moen, a sociology professor at the University of Minnesota. Developing common interest keeps relationship strong. One couple I know started a boutique baking business, selling cakes and desserts to upscale restaurants in Houston; another couple bought a cruise franchise and now plan trips for other retirees, with unlimited cruises for themselves. But be skeptical of franchise offers, as mentioned in my book, *Retirement is for Sissies* (Amazon.com), because the average 400 franchise cost cannot be recouped the first four years.
5. **Consider working for your kids**. This may sound strange, but many extended families have bonded together economically to offer mom and pop a part-time job that allows them to maintain their pre-retirement standard of living at the same time providing valuable mentoring to their children. This only works if your children own their own businesses and work conflict is avoided (remember your children are the

bosses). If you sold the business to your children, have a third-party design an exit strategy for yourself.
6. Finally, the most important lesson of all—**take time to smell the roses**. Work at a more leisurely pace: breakfast at 10 am, do not respond to crises, take time for fun and exercise, mentor the young, enjoy a long lunch, and take a 20-minute power nap.

It's no surprise that the top worries of retirees are: (not mutually exclusive) boredom (45%), sex and romance (45%), and intimations of mortality (34%), compared to pre-retirement employees: aggravation (30%), money (34%) and personal appearance (28%).

Helpful Hints:

1. Buy my book, *Retirement is for Sissies,* to gain additional insight that retirement is a myth. Work is an action verb for those who are adventurous, healthy, and spiritually connected.
2. If you're in your 30s and 40s, stay away from retirement seminars that focus only on money. Remaining a contributor to society rather than only a consumer changes one's perspective from present to future-oriented.
3. Instead of a retirement party, give yourself an "engagement" party to continue to enjoy life with a network of family and friends. Emotional health is key to enjoying your "retirement" years.

Who You Gonna' Call?

You've seen Arnie's commercials on TV: he's pulling for the small businessperson with the help of Administaff. While the analogy may seem a little far fetched, running your own business is easier if you have a coach to help you along the way. Of course if you were opening a golf club, Arnie would be my choice, but what if you were considering a career change from corporate America to *numero uno*? If you're like most of us, you might get the "yips" while putting a three-footer for the victory. If you will permit the golf metaphor I'd like to offer a few insights into why coaching rather than consulting might be the better play if you're thinking of going out on your own.

Coaching is *more* personal than consulting. There are many business consultants who can help you with a business plan, financial projections, inventory and personnel, and banking relationships. In golf, the club pro can give you lessons to improve your mechanics to perfect your game. A business consultant does the same thing—he/she works on your performance skills by increasing knowledge while taking into account your ability for the game (business). A coach, on the other hand, is like your personal caddy, who walks with you from tee to green mapping out each hole and pin location, checking yardage, terrain, and wind conditions to help build your self-confidence. Most CEOs have personal coaches who tackle the biggest obstacle of all—and that is, the space between their ears. It's been said that golf is a mental game and business is no different.

Let's see why a coach makes sense if you're moving from amateur to professional ranks in running your own business. First, you must give up the security of a salaried position with great benefits and paid vacation and sick days. Second, you give up a great staff who assists you in every aspect of your job: accounting, human resources, quality and risk management, operations, and a set of rules to play by. Third, you have the professional and social support of your colleagues to bounce ideas off if you are unsure of a decision. Fourth, you have a legal staff to protect your assets. There are many third-party administrators like Administaff who can handle all these functions with experience and expertise.

Sounds easy, but you're standing over a three-foot putt relying on only your knowledge, skills, and ability. Your business consultant is safely watching the game at home, managing your assets and investments, and keeping you out of trouble. But look behind you and whom do you see? Your caddy is the one who helped you read the green, measured the slope and speed of the putt, and gives you the confidence you need to drop the putt in the hole. Most professional golfers have "swing coaches" who perfect their swing when they're not striking the ball properly. In the same way, as a new business owner you want someone who understands YOU rather than your business.

Back to the golf analogy; your caddy travels with you from tournament to tournament—watching your practice rounds, workouts, and pre-game preparation. He gets inside your head to fill that space between your ears that's buried with self-doubt, overconfidence, miscalculations, or plain "stinkin' thinkin.'" A coach, likewise, becomes your *alter ego* to challenge your assumptions, prejudgments, biases, and mental game. As a coach, your caddy works on your timing, reaction, motivation, and physiologic responses in a high-stakes game where winning and losing can cost you your business, reputation, investment, and credibility.

So next time you see Arnie on TV espousing the benefits of having your own business consultant with you, remember the famous Ghostbuster's line: *who you gonna call*? Who you gonna call at 2 a.m. when you've got to meet payroll the next day and you've already maxed your line of credit with the bank? Who you gonna call when you have doubts about growing your business too rapidly and you can't keep up with new orders? Who you gonna call when you start second-guessing yourself after all the numbers make sense on your balance sheet?

I hope by now you see the difference between business *consulting* and business *coaching*. If you're to have a successful business venture, both individuals are needed, each with a necessary, but different skill set for you to succeed. So the next time you think about leaving the comfortable surrounds of your corner office, hire a business coach first to see if you have what it takes to manage the doubt and uncertainty of running your own business. Your family may believe you can do it, but your coach will ask the powerful questions so *you* believe you can do it.

Helpful Hints:

1. What is the primary difference between consulting and coaching?
2. Pick a time in your career when you needed coaching and why.
3. Re-read the chapter on coaching and the types of questions a coach would ask of you to clarify your reasons for improving job performance or changing careers.

Where Have All The Boomers Gone?

Harvard Management Update is an excellent resource for a $109 annual subscription; Weekly updates and Pod Casts are provided via iTunes on the latest thinking regarding business and industry. The latest article by Anne Field parallels a book I've written for Boomers (born 1947 to 1961) who are about to retire and wondering what they will do with their Type A personalities once they leave the workforce. The book is titled *Retirement is for Sissies,* by iUniverse.com and available on Amazon.com and BN.com.

The gist of Field's article is that at least 50% of executives in the USA will be eligible to retire in the next five years.* This normally would not pose a problem if it were not for Generation XY who have grown up in the computer age and have meager experience in process management and team-building. The leadership drain will affect not only the top levels of management but levels two, three, and four. So what's a company to do?

1. **Accelerate leadership development**. Don't rely on the traditional "trial by fire." Your company should have an executive development program that selects junior managers and grooms them for more senior positions as soon as they hire on.
2. **Get your junior executives coaching** and a mentor to give them the tools they will need to lead teams through difficult times of growth, downsizing, and change.
3. **Pick out your "star players"** and let them know they're being groomed for executive positions on a fast-track. Give them encouragement and keep them informed. Don't play "I've got a secret" with them or they will look elsewhere for promotions.

4. **Peer-group work**. Develop "high-performance" teams with explicit training in driving innovation, managing conflict, process management, and game simulations in senior leadership roles running hypothetical businesses. There are excellent training programs around the country. For more information visit Dr. Randi Smith's website, www.virtualgroupinstitute.com.
5. **Active learning project teams**. Expose folks to new areas in the business from a successful company leader who had has been a project leader for at least five years. What you want to do is connect the learning and development experience with what's actually going on in the business, according to Jennifer Harnden of Fidelity Investments.
6. Provide leadership training. This is basic, but true. Leadership skills can be learned. Among the more valuable skills are: adaptability, tolerance for uncertainty and conflict, relationship skills, the ability to step back and let your subordinates take over, and most important, self-awareness.

* Anne Field is a Pelham, NY business writer and can be reached at MUOpinion@hbsp.harvard.edu

Helpful Hints:

1. If you're a junior executive ask your boss for a mentor who has at least five years of project management experience and is willing to have you "shadow" him/her during the next three months.
2. Take a long-distance learning course on running high-performance teams. The University of Texas at Dallas School of Business has an excellent program.
3. Find a business coach who specializes in running process groups where adaptability, intuition, and self-awareness are important to team success.

Section Four: Economic Impact on Jobs and Coaching

Section Four addresses behavioral economics and the interplay of human emotion and economics, which has particular relevance in 2008 with the recent financial markets debacle. Individual companies and books are singled out that cut against the grain of greed and poor management. These companies are run by savvy CEOs with both a strategic and business plan to survive in an economic downturn. Chapters include: behavioral economics, the current economic state in 2008, the financial markets, industrial to cultural revolution, the luxury generation, energy consumption, 100 fastest growing companies, giving in the 21st century, wiring the medical world, Target's secret, Jack Welch's book, *Winning,* Malcolm Gladwell's book, *Blink,* and Peter Drucker.

Behavioral Economics

I owe the idea for this article from my good friend, Dan Kutsko, a physicist and teacher, who inspires his students to think "outside the box." He is also a student of history, astronomy, mathematics, and classical literature. He shared an article from an ongoing think tank called "The Edge" which is comprised of leading scholars around the world who focus on the intersection between probability theory, psychology, and economics. Led by Richard Thaler, the father of behavioral economics and the Director of the Center for Decision Research at the University of Chicago Graduate School of Business, he is coauthor (with Cass Sunstein) of *Nudge: Improving Decisions About Health, Wealth, and Happiness.* Other noted colleagues are: Sendhil Mullainathan, Professor of Economics at Harvard and Executive Director of Institute of Quantitative Social Science, and Daniel Kahneman, Professor of Psychology, Princeton University and Woodrow Wilson School of Public and International Affairs. He is also the winner of the 2002 Nobel Prize in Economic Sciences for his pioneering work in integrating insights about human judgment and decision-making under uncertainty, a timely topic given today's Stock Market and global economy.

Thaler offers four tenets for his foundations of behavioral economics: *bounded rationality, bounded selfishness, bounded self-control, and bounded arbitrage.* The first three bounds are self-evident and based on human behavior. The economic markets are able to exploit human folly, according to Thaler, which is why panic selling occurs in a down market (rather than buying) and vice versa in an up market. Bounded arbitrage has to do with the limits one is willing to compromise given risk-reward and duration in the markets. The longer the duration, the more the volatility and risk-reward; the less the time left for retirement, the lower the volatility and less the risk-reward, thus more conservative investments of liquidity. Social psychology can predict that humans fear loss more than we love gain; thus we are less willing to opt out of savings programs than opt-in (which is the current system). Also, people are influenced by money and tend to be more selfish and less willing to help others. Those who are skeptical of a more wholelistic and religious view of monetary envy being evil, tend to be more risk-aversive in their investments. Those who believe that money is no more than currency provided by providence with spiritual gifts of talents, skills, and abilities tend to be more risk-aversive and willing to share their money through philanthropy (witness the Gates Foundation and Warren Buffett).

Thaler talks about Econs and Humans. Humans are like Homer Simpson, while Econs are like Mr. Spock. Humans care about how a question is put to them that an Econ would identify as mathematically equivalent without emotion. Thaler has a concept called "libertarian paternalism" which is an Opt-In program such as save more tomorrow (SMT) for 401k plans. We don't generally save much, so his program allows us to save on the basis of promotions and raises, which means our standard of living remains relatively constant (a tough nut to crack for most humans). In fact we, as humans, opt-in for the "spend for tomorrow" program which is promulgated by credit card companies who get rich off our greed and selfishness. Before we know it, we're counting on bonuses to meet living expenses, and bankruptcy is right around the corner.

Sendhil argues that poor people exhibit similar behavior with food stamps and payday loans. His argument is that under scarcity there is a systematic effect that you put the discount rate way too high for our own good. Senhil's research concentrates on his native country of India where he studies fruit vendors who typically have debt payments from their profits, similar to credit card payments in the U.S. His argument is that busy folks behave similarly to poor folks: if you have little time, it is scarce and you are as time-poor as the fruit vendors in India. You commit to future events (raise, bonus, promotion, lottery) and act like there is no tomorrow while spending. The crux of this argument is that time cannot be borrowed or banked, so when the bank calls in your loan, we must default because we think we can bank time.

More discussion about behavioral economics will be discussed in future issues, but I direct your attention to www.edge.org for more information on this topic.

Helpful Hints:

1. Argue that monetary temptation is a regressive tax, while time temptation is a progressive tax.
2. Look at your present savings plan; to what extent do you ignore time constraints? What can you change in your spending and borrowing habits to lessen this gap?
3. Why do poor people contribute a greater percentage of their disposable income to charitable organizations and churches? How does Thaler's theory explain why such seemingly irrational behavior is, in fact, rational?

What's With The Economy?

Listening to the pundits causes us to believe that we're already in a recession—gas prices soaring, corn prices increasing for alternative fuels, food costs up. It's gloom and doom again as if we're headed into a another 1929-1933 economic depression. However, until the demand side of the economic equation changes we will continue to see higher prices. George Bush was in Palestine today trying to persuade them to increase supply to lower oil prices. He was met with indifference. He shouldn't have been surprised. The U.S. still pays a miniscule amount for gasoline per capita consumption compared to Europe and other parts of the world. Let me share with you some examples of consumer behavior that tells me we will continue to see soaring gas prices.

- SUVs and other V-8 muscle cars continue to dominate U.S. roadways. The three top selling vehicles are the BMW, Mercedes, and Lexus. Forget the hybrids; they remain an anomaly on the American roadways.
- People continue to fly despite jet fuel prices that have quadrupled over the last three years. Despite IT video-conferencing, meetings remain the dominate means of conducting business globally. The cost of doing business increases as the profit margins increase—guess who is paying for these increases? You and me every time we gas up.
- American technology continues to escalate exponentially as IPODs, IPhones, LEDs, microchips continue to decrease in price and consumers line up for the next new game platform and flat screen TV. Now HD DVD will become a standard in February, 2009, and Americans will have to convert to a digital signal if they already haven't. Pity the poor guy who

still receives a snowy picture with rabbit ears and aluminum foil.
- Despite health care advances we let drug companies continue to bombard us with pills for every ailment from erectile dysfunction to acid reflux. We now have "the purple pill," the "blue pill," the "pink pill" the "butterfly pill" because drug companies must push the illness model rather than the wellness model and doctors are reduced to "pill pushers." Again consumer drug costs rise exponentially compared to the CPI because drug companies create a "false demand" for medication.
- If you ever find yourself at a drive-thru again (take my word, don't go there) how many times does the person ask you if you want twelve other items besides your salad? Another example of consumerism masquerading as consumer demand.
- And what's with the sports apparel industry? Do we have to have matching workout clothes to look our best as we sweat in the gym? And what's with the logos? Does the little "checkmark" give you and advantage or just put more money in the other guy's pocket. Besides sweat you're giving up dollars in the gym. And who needs a personal trainer after three months? If you haven't figured out the machines yet, then take up walking. It's better for you unless you want to pay your orthopedic surgeon for your next rotator cuff surgery because your insatiable desire to lift more weight.
- So as we go through the DJIA I've touched on transportation, apparel, energy, entertainment, and technology. Next time the Dow takes a dive look at how much your spending on needless "stuff" and ask yourself, "do I feel lucky, yet?" (thanks and apologies to my man, Clint).

Helpful Hints:

1. Take out your checkbook or credit card statement now and look at your last variable expenses. Did you absolutely have

to spend that money (need) or did you make an impulse purchase because of greed and ease of credit? (want)
2. Next time you clean out your closet and give to Goodwill or other notable charity, do you go out and replace your clothing? If you do, you haven't learned the basic axiom of supply and demand.
3. Do you contribute to a retirement program? If you do, you're lucky, even if you are self-employed. Cut demand and prices will go down. Just look at last year's bestsellers on the bargain table for $4.95.

The Financial Markets

Okay, you've heard the news from both political candidates about our woeful financial crisis and there is cause for concern—i.e. a 700 Billion dollar bail-out for Fannie and Freddie; an 85 Billion bail-out for AIG, Barclays saves Lehman Brothers on the heels of former brokerage collapses on Wall Street. Who's minding the store? The Democrats would say "no one." All Bush appointees are clueless and didn't see the train wreck coming; Republicans blame a democratic Congress who vetoed reforms to increase regulation on banks and lending institutions in 2005. Whoever is responsible isn't owning up to it, and we, the tax payers are footing the bill to the tune of $2400 per tax payer.

Let's look at a few basic management principles. **Number one is leadership** (or lack thereof). Remember the Enron debacle and Ken Lay telling stockholders holding worthless paper that "don't worry, a turnaround is coming." Reminds me of Alfred E. Newman of *Mad Magazine*—"what, me worry?" The chair of the Securities and Exchange Commission (SEC) should be regulating and setting monetary policy. Instead, we are using tax payer money to shore up bungling and incompetent leadership who are raking in *billions* of dollars in compensation before the house of cards collapses. The S&L crisis of the 90s was similar in that loans were being made without sufficient personalized collateral and greed again was the culprit as evidenced by the Charles Keating debacle. Leaders are paid to keep current on what's going on inside their companies; if Enron taught us anything it's that "dummy books" are illegal and unethical and draws a wedge between the haves and have-nots.

Number two is management (or lack thereof), especially the regulatory part which is generally left to internal auditors who are paid by the company they work for. It's like the fox watching the hen house. Anyone who has worked IA knows that they are unpopular within the organization. Everyone runs when they see them coming and reports often end up collecting dust in the CEO's office. Furthermore the Board of Directors are kept in the dark and provided a set of "Teflon books" that erroneously suggests that "everything is well in Kansas." Management should be an active verb, not a noun. CEOs often leave the mechanics of running the daily operations to a COO who depends on VPs whose job it is to report accurately up the chain what's going on. CEOs should concentrate more on daily operations and leave the strategic planning and external factors to the "planners and outside consultants" who are in a dotted relationship to the CEO. This gives your consultants the freedom they need to make recommendations without political fall-out or recourse from the company (unless their contract is not renewed).

Number three is to remain current with technology but not at the expense of your customers. IT should be a support function and should not drive your business. It's nice to give your customers "more bang for the buck" but technology is cyclical and the information should be supportive of the company's strategic plan including vision and values statements. Timeframes should be 3-5 years and include measureable goals on how to position your company in a competitive market. If you are a financial lending institution, then how are you going to draw and keep customers, beyond the ads and promises of "friendly customer service?"

The most important variable for financial markets is "volatility," which has to do with the risk-benefit of one's investment. Are you dealing with individual or institutional investors? Do you stress both income and dividends as in most balanced funds? If you are in a large growth fund you need to look at 1, 3, 5, and 10 year average returns. Also one's portfolio should be diversified using income-averaging investing (a certain amount invested each month for the long-term), rather than short-term investing. If you're in individual stocks you should know something about the companies you invest in such as K-1s and other financial data from Moody or other reputable watchdog company. Stay away from commodities, derivatives, and junk bonds. If you're in a mutual fund look at the volatility ratings of the different funds. In current economic times it's better to be in a balanced than a growth fund; to have more liquidity such as municipal and federally insured bonds. The closer you are to retirement (3-5 years) the more liquid your funds should be.

So back to the hysteria on Wall Street. My advice is that if you are not going to retire or withdraw your retirement funds in the next two years that you wait out the current bear market and have a preset plan to re-distribute your funds into more liquid assets at a certain level of the market—e.g. 12,000 DOW or some other index. The market will correct itself after the panic selling ceases. I look for an upturn in January after a new President is sworn into office.

Helpful Hints:

1. Review your portfolio with your financial advisor at least twice a year, but no more than quarterly. Consider his/her advice with your own judgment of the markets and social psychology on crowd contagion behaviors.
2. Invest long-term (more than ten years) in upcoming "green technology" which was reported in a previous newsletter; invest short-term (less than three years) in balanced funds and bonds.
3. Develop a 3-5 year investment plan for yourself and review it annually. In your plan consider the following: market strengths and weaknesses, external opportunities and threats, vision and mission statements, values clarification, business strategies and key strategies for reaching them, goals, and action plans.

From Industrial to Cultural Revolution

"Lean and mean," is the motto of many American corporations today. Labor is cheaper in China, Pakistan, India, and Central America, and our Fortune 500 companies are taking advantage of cost-cutting to remain competitive in a global market. Let's look at automobiles. China is capable of making a 12k automobile that would rival Japan's #1 car in America, Toyota, but trade tariffs and social and political issues keep Chinese automobiles from competing with American cars and other imports. High on the list of U.S. grievances is China's human rights violations and communist government that allows for working children in what amounts to slave wages and incarceration in factories, reminiscent of the garment industry in the 1900s in NYC.

Politicians are uneasy to point out that over seven billion dollars are leaving our country each year to fund other nations in energy, manufacturing, and software design. Some of these dollars do not leave paper trails and much of the money is wired into Swiss banks for re-distribution into foreign currencies that fare much better than the U.S. dollar, further draining our economy. America ingenuity that defined our country in the 60s and 70s is losing ground because small business cannot compete with the tax advantages given to big business. Witness the latest joint Chinese-American manufacturing company, *Haier*, that manufactures refrigerators in Camden, South Carolina. Although employing only 128 South Carolinians, *Haier* employs over 50,000 workers in 16 countries with an annual growth rate of 68% from 1985 to 2005 (from www.expansionmanagement.com). Economic incentives allowed for cheap land, low taxes, and non-secured loans to launch a business that competes with *Whirlpool* and *Kenmore*. The payback for Americans is for low-middle income workers to continue employment and keep their homes after the massive layoffs because of the textile industry being outsourced to China. China now exports almost 3,000 goods to America and other countries around the world. The industrial revolution of the 1900s has given way to the Cultural Revolution in the 21st century.

Fortune magazine describes a major shakeup in our global economy by publishing the latest figures on the "Global 500." To make this list, companies must earn $16.7 billion in revenues which is up 12% from last year. U.S. companies make up only 153, the fewest in over a decade, in large part due to the declining U.S. dollar. Brazil, Russia, and India did quite well, thanks to oil and mining metals. China is stealing the show with Sinopec ranked at No. 16 this year, with another 28 companies on the 500 list. In fact, China posted as many companies as Italy, Spain, and Australia combined. India's Tata Steel (No. 315) garnered $25.7 billion in sales with a phenomenal 353% increase from last year.

The U.S. has 8 of the top 25 listings with Wal-Mart and Exxon-Mobil heading the list. China has three (16-Sinopec, 24-State Grid, and 25-China National Petroleum). Trade agreements become critical in a global economy and the U.S. must reverse the flow of dollars outside our borders to Europe, Asia, and South America. The middle class is being squeezed out and American business is doing very little to reverse this trend. Just last month Detroit gave pink slips to over 1,000 middle managers at GM. Foreclosures are up, food prices are up, gas prices are returning just below $2 nationally from a high of $5 last quarter. One-third of Americans cannot afford health insurance and bankruptcies have hit a record high. Yes, we have the war in Iraq and American lives to protect, but we can't do it on the backs of middle-class Americans who have fought in at least three wars on foreign soil and are wasting away in Veterans hospitals and nursing homes on Medicaid and federal assistance. Yet, our Congressmen receive free health care for their family members. Ask any small business person with 50 or fewer employees and ask what they pay for health care and the rates are drastic because there is no larger employee pool to aggregate their health risks. That's why many who work for small businesses either go without health insurance or pay exorbitant rates in a "high risk" pool.

It's time for "Made in America" to mean something again. Let's not trade quality for education and training of U.S. workers. We need to fix our educational system and develop a vocational track for those students who wish to enter the manufacturing workforce earlier without penalty of losing their jobs or advancement through job incentives to further their education. I would also ask that international partnerships (much along the lines of Toyota) be formed that benefit both the U.S. and foreign countries without penalizing the U.S. It's no secret that most of our new patents are from the United States and royalties should accrue to those companies who produced the patents. China has a notorious track record of stealing patents and copyright infringement that has not been adequately addressed by the two previous Presidents.

Helpful Hints:

1. Google "global economy" and see how many foreign countries have advanced over the last decade and increasing their GNP.
2. The next time you go into a electronics store see if you can find any U.S. companies as brand names on TVs, computers, electronic accessories.
3. Ask your next-door neighbor if he/she is better off economically than they were eight years ago.

The Luxury Generation

The "me" generation of the 60s has given way to the "Luxury Generation" as Boomers today flock to exclusive brands to define them as a generation apart from earlier generations. True we didn't grow up in the depression of the 30s. True our parents were part of the *Greatest Generation* as Tom Brokaw wrote about two years ago. True we are more self-reliant than our parents who depended on neighbors to help when times were tough. True we spoiled our children rotten with every conceivable gadget that now produces not only exclusivity but solitude, social retardation, and obesity. To say *gauche* would be an understatement. Suitcases that start at 5k in white leather that would tear easily if handled by a commercial airline.

A brief history of "classploitation" as coined by Peter Gumbel in *Fortune* includes:

- *Pierre Cardin* in 1960 with licensing of his ready to wear outfits for women
- *Cartier* launches the gold lighter in 1968 that became the standard for the rich and famous
- *Louis Vuitton* in 1987 with the merger with *Moet Hennessy* into LVMH
- *Gucci* injects sex appeal into clothing design in 1990
- *Calvin Klein* uses scantily clad teens to display his unisex underwear in 1992
- *Dior* brands handbags displayed by celebrities, including Princess Diana in 1995
- *Courvoisier* opens as a movie in a SNL spoof in 2000
- *Karl Lagerfeld* becomes the first big name producer of a Swedish retailer H&M in 2004
- *Oprah* Winfrey announces she'll never buy *Hermes* after refused entry at closing in 2005

- *Prada* introduces its designer cell phone in 2007

Where do you think our kids get the idea for *Abercrombie and Fitch, Hollister*, and other name brands? In the 50s *The Man in the Gray Flannel Suit* described the dress code for a generation of men who worked away from home. Advertising and branding are big business that has propelled Chief Marketing Officers (CMOs) to the pinnacle of their corporations to perpetuate excess to define a generation of exclusivity and snobbery. Turn on the radio and one hears Jim Nance talk about Rolexes, buy that $220k Vuitton Tourbillon watch and your company will place your zodiac sign on it, or you can have a limited edition of 100 bottles of cognac at $200k a bottle.

I'm afraid I don't understand this "luxury" business. Why the compulsion to define who we are by what we wear, drink, drive, and vacation? The *Noveau Riche* must make their mark on a world that is defined by the "haves and have-nots."

My other pet peeve is the global warming advocates who count "carbon footprints" like one would DNA sequences; yet, they continue to live in 10k square foot homes, consuming gas and electricity at alarming rates, as they lecture the masses who can barely pay their electric bills for their sub-prime mortgage first homes. The 21st Century has elevated snobbery to a sordid level of greed and entitlement. In an age of "spiritual enlightenment" where 82% of Americans state they believe in God, we also have the highest poverty rates of any industrialized nation. Despite the shining examples of Warren Buffet and Bill and Melinda Gates, corporate sleaze has sunk to new lows as evidenced by the Enron debacle in 2000. Other nations view us as gluttons, egomaniacs, and voracious consumers of precious limited resources. It's time to not buy into the myth that "excess is better." If we are to gain any credibility with our neighboring nations, then we must shift the spending paradigm to "frugality is not for the foolish." Our nation is not a nation of "savers" but "spenders." The bumper sticker that we are spending our children's inheritances sadly depicts the "me" generation today. Our parents would truly be disappointed in our lack of stewardship.

Helpful Hints:

1. Check out the ads in any magazine and notice that money buys distinction.
2. Why has the leisure industry prospered and look to whom they market? We've gone from weeks to points; from gold to platinum to diamond credit cards: from conservation to propagation of our excessive need to define ourselves by material possessions.
3. Explain why charitable contributions continue to decline in an age of prosperity.

Energy Consumption

According to *USA Today* this month clean tech start-ups were the second fastest growing companies after software. Venture capitalists are quick to infuse over 800 million dollars to find cleaner and cheaper alternative fuels while also preserving our environment. Despite being labeled "greenees" by the oil and gas companies there is now technology to convert food products (i.e. corn) into ethanol. Our hybrids now run on 85% ethanol which is significantly more fuel efficient than the standard 10% ethanol found in our refined gas today.

Despite the political rhetoric about becoming energy independent from foreign oil the major oil companies aren't about to raise significant capital for more refineries or alternative energy sources. Let's face it: oil companies are here to make money and as long as demand exceeds international supply of fuels, gasoline prices will continue to rise. China and Japan are driving up prices because of their high demand for oil and gas which they can afford given that their standard sedans start around 12k dollars. The U.S. is not about to let China import more fuel efficient and cheaper cars into the U.S. because domestic production will decrease further. GM has already announced over 1000 layoffs, mostly middle managers. Although larger V-8 SUVs are languishing in used car lots, Americans are not about to give up their Japanese cars which get more than 30 mpg. Hybrids will have to reduce costs before mom and pop leave their Chevy pickup in the driveway. And don't forget about our newest teenage drivers who still prefer performance and looks to fuel efficiency.

Now what about burning more coal? We're told that we've got another 100-year supply of coal buried beneath our continent, and dirty technology is ready and willing to extract the coal and pour CO^2 and methane vapors into the air. If we want to disregard EPA standards and health risks then some energy folks say coal is the way to go—it's cheaper, more available, and easier to refine. Forget about windmills and solar energy. The West Coast elite can keep their fancy cars and need not worry about $5 a gallon gas. T. Boon Pickens has come out with his own energy plan which talks about retrofitting our existing refineries to increase output. And then we have former House Speaker, Newt Gingrich who wants to "drill more and drill now." All these short-sighted supply-side approaches overlook the basic problem of American consumption and our refusal to consider alternative sources of transportation and energy.

What about waste products? We now have the technology to turn waste products into fuel. Remember John Travolta in the movie *Phenomenon*? He had figured out a way to convert garbage into electricity by using refuse and manure to grow vegetables. What about nuclear energy? Despite the fact that France is 80% nuclear in energy production, the U.S. still remembers three-mile Island in New York and the fear of nuclear fall-out. The *Simpsons* TV show and movie features Homer who has had several near nuclear accidents, which plays on U.S. fears around an energy source they can't see, feel, or touch. I think it will be a while before nuclear generators dot our landscapes more than land fills.

So how do we solve the energy crisis at home? I have a four-part plan: 1) car pool or buy a scooter; 2) use solar and wind energy; 3) increase our reliance on nuclear energy; 4) go with clean tech in waste conversion to energy fuels. Let's get rid of our complete dependence on fossil fuels by getting rid of our fossil politicians in Washington.

Helpful Hints:

1. Research the latest technology in converting waste products to fuels. We can get rid of the land fills and toxic wastes.
2. Next time you spend $100 on filling up your SUV, think about a scooter or public transportation.
3. Electric cars are probable in the next 10 years. *Testa* already has a prototype roadster that can power up to 125 mph and runs on a rechargeable battery pack.

Small Business: 100 Fastest Growing Companies

Fortune Small Business (FSB) magazine lists the 100 fastest growing companies for 2006. The magazine is a favorite among small business owners who employ less than 50 employees. Most new companies are found in Texas (14) and by sector, they comprise: manufacturing (25), casino and gaming (2), restaurants and food services (4), consumer products (4), telecom (5), healthcare administration (10), energy (11), healthcare (11), technology (18), and other (10).

The small-cap sector is where fast new companies enter the marketplace, but it's also risky business. Most have market caps of 500 million and are thinly traded with high volatility. Investments in these companies are risky business, but the rewards can be great. Let's take a look at a sample from this year's list.

Fuel Tech's growth (#12) is fueled by "dirty business," literally. They deal in slag removal technology which boosts energy plant efficiency and reduces emissions at coal plants. Fuel Tech injects a chemical cocktail into boilers with increased revenues of 42% and stock tripled to $30. With over 1500 coal plants just in the U.S. the demand is unlimited. China, India, and Mexico are keenly interested in the technology which uses a computerized model of fire to know exactly where to spray the compound into boilers similar to milk of magnesia into a fire.

The Knot (#15) was an IPO in 2000 with its stock tanking to 42 cents and delisted from NASDAQ. The company's founders took advantage of web ads and founded their own magazine to acquire Wedding Pages, a regional wedding magazine publisher. The husband-wife team also founded The Nest and magazine for newly weds and Nest Baby. They may continue the life cycle and follow the married couple through Empty Nest and Retirement.

Rocky Mountain Chocolate (#80) is the largest chocolate retailer in terms of locations surpassing Godiva and See's. He sells in over 44 states in resort towns which cater to those on vacation who are not interested in watching their diet. Founded by Frank Crail in Durango, Colorado he has become the "Candy Man," with profits climbing 17% and revenues last year of 4.7 million. He gets 250,000 for each franchise he opens plus royalties and hopes to open another 40 stores in 2007.

United Therapeutics (#22), based in Silver Spring, Md., reported 159 million in revenues last year. The company makes and sells Remodulin, a drug that treats pulmonary hypertension in arteries that supply the lungs. The founder, Martine Rothblatt, an attorney, launched her biotech firm in 1996 to treat her daughter who battled this rare disease. Originally injected under the skin, the drug is now taken IV and clinical trials begin on oral tablets later this year.

For a complete listing of the 100 companies go to *FSB*'s July/August 2007 issue.

Helpful Hints:

1. Go to www.zachs.com, an investment research firm to see computer models that track SEC data to find trends in small company growth.
2. Look at the NASDAQ for small-cap companies and look at P/E ratios to see investment opportunities; historical stock prices will give you a sense at volatility and risk potential.
3. Newly started healthcare companies take advantage of private equity firms and "angel investors" to partner with major pharmaceutical companies and biotech firms to diagnose and treat common diseases such as hypertension and diabetes. "Better mousetraps" are the name of the game in this arena.

Giving in the 21ˢᵗ Century

When Warren Buffet announced that he would commit his wealth to the Bill and Melinda Gates Foundation, he set a new standard for philanthropy—over 41 billion dollars tied to his Hathaway Empire in stock dividends and cash advances. Buffet has appointed each of his children to head up a different philanthropic endeavor and they will be handsomely paid by non-profit standards, but far less than they would make in the corporate world.

In the current issue of *Fortune*, Melinda Gates adorns the front cover with the byline: The 100 Billion Dollar Woman (kind of a take off on the hit TV show in the 80s, the 7 million dollar man). Rumor has it that her husband Bill will work full-time to assist his wife in doling out money to worldly projects from Aids/HIV in Africa to tuberculosis and malaria and world hunger. In fact, Steve Ballmer replaced Melinda's husband in 2000 to prep him for the tougher task of spending the billions that their foundation will reap over the next twenty years.

The Gates' Foundation receives 6000 grant requests annually and Melinda reads each request. Their total 2006 commitments were 2.7 billion dollars. The Gates' Foundation has allied themselves with NIH, Michael and Susan Dell, GlaxoSmithKline and Proctor & Gamble to form a joint venture the Global Alliance for Vaccines and Immunization (GAVI) to help developing nations fight childhood diseases. They also help the USA with their educational initiatives for early learning, scholarships, advocacy, school computers where some 70% of 9ᵗʰ graders do not graduate on time

But the Gates are not alone in their philanthropy. Other heavyweights include: Larry Brilliant of Google who oversees some $2 billion dollars from Google's founders, Larry Page and Sergey Brin to fight poverty, reverse global warming and help the world's most vulnerable patients. Interesting, Google's philanthropic efforts are not set up as a non-profit to escape various IRS restrictions and can make investments more quickly.

Jeff Lug and Jeffrey Sachs have formed the Millennium Promise to reduce global poverty by the years 2015. They have already raised more than $100 million and are partnering with companies like GE, Novartis, Ericsson to assist over 80 African villages. Jeff Flug worked for Goldman Sachs for 20 years while Sachs worked as an economist.

Everyone knows what Michael J. Fox has done for Parkinson's disease. He has testified before Congress, enlisted the help of Hollywood and US corporations to spend more than $100 million on research on Parkinson's and other neurological disorders.

Jacqueline Novogratz, Founder, Acumen Fund has invested over $27 million in 18 businesses in Asia and Africa; you might have seen their nets commercial on TV to fight malaria in Tanzania. Their consumers number four billion people who make less than $2 a day.

Techies Pierre Omidyar (eBay founder) and Matt Bannick have formed the Omidyar network to solve social problems and has already committed $120 million to give kids school supplies.

George Dayton, Target's founder over 60 years ago began investing 5% of his pretax profits for helping others. Today Target funds over $150 million annually in donated food, museum and theater tickets for school programs across America.

Make-up giant, MAC (a division of Estee Lauder) who makes Viva Glam lipstick donates 100% of his revenue to AIDS and has raised $100 million since 1994, making it the largest corporate HIV/AIDS donor outside the pharmaceutical companies.

J.D. Hoye and Sandy Weill (former CEO of Citigroup) and Ken Chenault (CEO of American Express) have trained more than 50,000 teens in financial services, hospitality, and IT industries since 1982.

In summary, it's refreshing to know that corporate greed is a cheap shot and that private capital can fight world problems. In reality it's more fun to spend money than to make it and the corporate givers mentioned in *Fortune* magazine have hired top-notch epidemiologists, researchers, philanthropists, and financial advisors to help them reach as many people around the world as possible. It may take a village to help a country, but these heavyweight venture capitalists are turning their attention to social and health issues long ago identified by the World Health Organization.

Helpful Hints:

1. Next time you check out at a Target store remember that 5% of your purchase goes to helping financially needy children in school.
2. The Greed of the 80s portrayed by Michael Douglas in the movie, *Wall Street* has been replaced by a new breed of corporate raider who looks much like Robin Hood.
3. For more corporate givers, go to www.Fortune.com/philanthropy.

Wiring the Medical World

McKesson is the largest healthcare services company and their CEO Hammergren and CIO Sprat are poised to revolutionize how medical information is collected from patients and conveyed electronically over the Internet. Although McKesson's business is distributing pharmaceuticals, the company wants to put health records on the information highway—a controversial subject that must balance patient right to privacy with better operating efficiency and effectiveness for hospitals, clinics, and doctors' offices.

Medical services is big business consuming 17% of our GDP and rising according to *Fortune's* Geoff Colvin's interview with McKesson's executives in the February, 2007 issue. According to Hammergren and Sprat it's "really not a technological issue, but one of adoption: are people ready for this?" Given HIPPA regulations and patient rights, EAPs, employee health data being available on computer for management and insurance companies who fund employee healthcare programs, greater accessibility to patient information incurs inherent risks with regard to the data being misused. One only needs to be reminded of the Daniel Elsberg incident during the Nixon presidency where the psychiatrist's office was broken into looking for important information on a U.S. congressman. Conceivably with the right password one might be able to hack into your medical chart and review your medications, diagnoses, and medical notes about your condition including information that could damage work status.

One area that is already being implemented is the dispensing of patient medication in hospitals using a wristband with a barcode that delivers the right medication at the right time to the right patient. Medication errors account for longer hospital stays and sometimes deaths. The computer element has reduced medication errors primarily due to inaccurate charting and illegible writing that must be accurately transposed from the doctor's note on the patient's chart to the pharmacy, back to the nurses' station, then to the attending nurse, and finally to the patient. McKesson estimates that over 300 thousand medication errors are caught weekly with the advanced computer tracking systems that can save many lives.

It comes as no surprise that computerization is part of doing business in almost every other industry except medicine. Spratt says "if you walk into any grocery store anywhere in the U.S., the same loaf of bread is going to get scanned the same way. But less than 20% of hospitals have a fully bar-coded medication-dispensing system. The biggest obstacle to implementing a fully electronic medical record are the doctors. Although physicians appreciate quick access to patient information, especially in emergencies, they are reluctant to give up control (and personal liability) to a system accessible to utilization review teams, peer review, and other hospital staff. This is not about paranoia, but the doctor's professional judgment being placed on the information highway for all to see and second guess including the patients and their families.

It comes as no surprise that doctors and hospitals are now ranked by US News & World Reports by specialty care, medication errors, patient deaths, etc. in gross, opinionated surveys with questionable validity. Now the computer has the potential to compare hospitals and doctors, just like you would car safety. This makes for an interesting debate in the medical and information technology fields with more debate in the future. But rest assured that McKesson will be at the forefront pushing for greater reliability and accountability in healthcare services.

Helpful Hints:

1. Next time you visit your doctor notice the computer in the patient room and ask how much of your medical record is available to clinic staff and what happens to that information.

2. Medication errors cost hospitals millions of dollars in litigation and good will to the community. Would you want a computer dispensing your IV meds or a nurse checking in on you every 30 minutes?
3. If you were going in for heart surgery would you want to know how many died of surgical complications and why? What's the best way to gain access to patient information: calling your doctor or looking it up on a website?

* From Ram's Rules in *Fortune's* February, 2008 magazine, pages 54-56.

Target's Secret

Fortune features Target's successful innovation tools that have propelled them from a dry goods store in Dayton, Ohio in 1903 to #33 of *Fortune's* Top 500 Companies. Two of nine top executives are women: Jodee Kozlak, EVP of Human Resources and Karen Gershman, SVP of Marketing. Target even has a VP for Strategy, Innovation and Insights, William Setliff. The "Red Bulls Eye" is recognized around the world and now appears on a white bulldog. Talk about Branding with a capital **B**.

Target's operating margins have increased from 5.4% to 8.6% in the last ten years. The stock has returned 795% since its IPO compared with 284% for the S&P retail index and 354% for Wal-Mart. The timeline for their phenomenal success since 1903 looks like a bullet train with the following cursory stops: 1956, the world's first enclosed shopping center in Dayton; 1962, the first Target store opens in Roseville, MN, the same year that Wal-Mart and Kmart launch; 1968, the Target Logo Bulls-eye appears; 1969 Dayton merges with J.L. Hudson to form Dayton Hudson; 1984, Robert Ulrich is named Target Stores president, a position he holds today, as CEO and chairman; 1995, first Super Target opens in Omaha; 2000, Dayton Hudson renamed Target Corporation; 2003, Target overtakes Wal-Mart in same-store sales growth; 2006, Target launches Go International fashion collections; 2008, Ulrich announces he will retire in May, to be replaced by Target president Gregg Steinhafel.

Target's slogan, "expect more, pay less," is catchy, but true. Their store designs have wider aisles for easier access to clothing and accessories, unlike the overcrowding at Wal-Mart with their high shelves and oversized carts. Target continues to open 100 stores annually with each store at one-sixth the size of Wal-Mart to provide easier access to fashion merchandise, like Converse, woven handbag from Loeffler Randall, Target's new cereal box, ITSO storage system, designers Erin Fetherston and Isaac Mizrahi.

2008 may be a momentous year with the change at the helm with Ulrich's departure, but the store chain has top-notch candidates for any succession scenario. Ulrich's leaving has been compared to Sam Walton's retirement from Wal-Mart in 1988 and Jack Welch's departure from General Electric in 2001. But Target's real advantage is not its CEO or logo, line of designer purses or catch slogan—it's the team that created them and there are 150 in-house managers primed and ready to replace them as part of their long-range strategic plan.

Helpful Hints:

1. Merchandising is tough business. How many bankruptcies and mergers resulting in department store disappearances can you name besides Bradlees, Venture, Caldor, Rose's, and Woolworth?
2. The secret to Target's success is succession planning and managerial training. What other industries contribute money and time to leadership development?
3. Niche buying is another secret to Target's success. Can you think of other retail stores that rely on *both volume and niche?*

A Review: Winning, by Jack Welch

I'd like to review Jack Welch's latest offering and *NY Times* Bestseller, *Winning*, written with his second wife, Suzy Welch, who I feel softened the old man up a little bit. His premise is simple, but right on: forget management theory, the only way to learn how to manage is to roll up your sleeves and do it. The medical profession has known this for years with their "see one, do one, teach one" training approach. Every medical student has learned this way in spite of what the books say. Unfortunately our management library is replete with "how to" books and esoteric theories that sound good but seldom are put in practice.

Make no mistake about it. Welch's book is a "take no prisoners" approach on how to run a successful company which he did at GE for forty years. His philosophy is simple: you win or you lose. It reminds me of John Wayne as a platoon sergeant in *Iwo Jima*, "See that hill men, let's take it." No namby-pamby. Welch ran GE the same way. Let's look at his take on "Mission Statements." This is clearly top management's responsibility. Don't delegate this to some Big Four management consulting company. If your leaders don't have a vision for the company, then replace them. Effective mission statements should balance the possible and the impossible (Welch, p. 15). Values are the *how* of the mission and should be specific and change behavior. Welch uses Bank One's values as an example of how to treat each other: 1) leaner is better; 2) eliminate bureaucracy; 3) cut waste relentlessly; 4) operations should be fast and simple; 5) value each other's time; 6) invest in infrastructure; and 7) we should know our customers best. How often do we spend in endless, repetitive meetings that have nothing to do with the above values? Welch would say if you've got time to gab, then take a cab. Another paraphrase might be, if you can't manage, then get the hell out of the way. Yes, he is coarse; yes, he is ego-driven; yes, he can be "in your face." But one thing you can't argue is GE's numbers: until recently the most profitable company in the world and leader of jet engines (Exxon-Mobil has surpassed with the recent upsurge in oil and gas prices).

Another hallmark is Welch's 20-70-10 rule. The top 20% are your "winners." Pay them handsomely so they don't leave. Pamper them if you have to; look at what George Steinbrenner's done with the NY Yankees. Welch uses the baseball metaphor often in his book and considers the top performers your "star players." The middle 70% are the backbone of the company and should not be ignored. Without middle management no one is left to do the hard work to design, build, and sell jet engines. The bottom 10% have been hitting below 200 for years and no longer need to take up space on the company's bench; *cut them; let them go; do them a favor* (and yourself); *adios*. He devotes a full chapter in giving the bad news to under-performers, in his chapter: "Letting Go is Hard to Do." First, no surprises, second, minimize humiliation. All good managers must do the dirty work of firing for non-performance. To ignore this is to ignore your responsibilities as a manager and you might be on the losing end at your next 360 evaluation.

I especially liked Welch's chapter on "Strategy: It's all in the sauce." Forget the fancy templates and power points. Strategy means making clear-cut choices about how to compete." (Welch, p.169). It's the SWOT analysis redefined in one sentence. Short, sweet, and simple. That's Jack Welch. In his chapter on "Getting Promoted: Sorry, No Shortcuts," he talks about: treat your subordinates like you would your boss, champion the company's major projects early on, search out and relish the input of mentors, and have a positive attitude and spread it around. There's one no-no: don't manage down. You've seen or worked for this person: s(he) is always telling you what the boss wants without buying into the mandate but only acting as the messenger. In other words, no backbone, no responsibility, no ownership, and no values, except "protect your own backside." Welch puts these managers in the bottom 10% who are on their way out the door.

Whether you love or hate this guy, *Winning* is entertaining and written to incite and debate the merits of managing people to produce winners. After all, who wants to work for a *losing* company? *Avis* branded itself as being No. 2 but look what it did for *Hertz*.

Helpful Hints:

1. Pick out a "how to" book that follows your passion: gardening, managing, writing, painting, to see if the charisma of the author was a factor in your selecting this book.
2. Look at how you respond to stress at work; ask your staff if they will share in a "no holds barred" encounter on whether you try to protect or infect staff with stress.
3. Ask yourself this question: Why do I work? Write a least 500 words and review if you work for extrinsic or intrinsic reasons.

Book Review: Blink

Much has been written about Malcolm Gladwell's book, *Blink*, about how to size up others and how we make snap judgments about others based on more than just intuition; it involves a series of intricate decisions based on neuroscience and psychology. Rather than review the neuroscience here I would like to review some applicable examples on how this works on a more practical level. Let's take the case of a successful sales person who has three rules: 1) treat the customer fairly 2) treat the customer fairly, and 3) treat the customer fairly. It's no secret that success is built on fairness, equity, and consistency. Customer satisfaction is critical to repeat business and referrals whether one is delivering a product or service. If you focus on your customer and pretend that you are the customer how would you want to be treated?

The best managers and sales staff are good active listeners. They are quiet and reserved, do not make assumptions, and let the customer tell them what they want. Let's suppose you want to buy a new car. You've done your homework, have a good idea of what you want to pay; don't want any runaround or games. Who would you rather deal with—a fast-talking, verbose salesperson who is a "know it all" or a sedate, quiet, knowledgeable salesperson who asks the right questions to narrow down your choice and price range. After all, buying a car is a "business" transaction, not a circus. It should not be a marathon with asking four people above the salesperson who have the authority to make the deal you want.

There is no such thing as mind reading—only good listening. Most people will tell you exactly what they want and you can either help them or refer them to someone else who might have a better product-client fit. One doesn't want to lose a contract or sale, but "service marketing" is a concept penned by Dr. Ben Dean twenty

years ago when he got into coaching, and he's built an entire coaching school based on this simple principle. Essentially, what I mean by service marketing is:
1. Give something of value to the customer.
2. Help the customer achieve what he/she wants for their money.
3. Go the extra mile in terms of service to the customer.
4. Give something extra that the customer doesn't expect—I call this the "wow" factor.

The above also works in relationships. If the couple is no longer talking to one another it's hard to make a connection and build intimacy. Communication is the key to building a good relationship in business, with family, or with friends. The "Golden Rule" applies in any situation if you want to be successful.

If you walk into a car dealership, look for the following: service awards given by their national trade association, friendly but not pushy sales staff who are knowledgeable and courteous. Look for clean restrooms, free coffee and soft drinks, snack food, reading area, good lighting, a roomy showroom, folks working and not loitering around, professional demeanor and dress, and most importantly, follow-up with the customer whether or not they purchased a vehicle from you.

Another concept worth mentioning is "thin slicing" which is what Gladwell refers to as slicing memory chips from the adaptive unconscious that leads to decisions based on experience. If we take the car buying illustration above, the astute sales person will size up a customer based on the last 100 customers he/she has met during their career and look for a "goodness of fit" between the new customer and past customers who have bought or passed on buying a vehicle in the past. It might be their walk, how they approach the sales staff, or how they react when approached by sales staff. Other indicators might be: sticker shock, use of the restroom and snack area, whether or not the entire family came for the car buying experience or just the husband or wife and husband, or wife only. Our brain acts like a binary computer where this information is fed into our frontal cortex and a "thin slice" or "snapshot" is taken of your potential customer and an informed judgment is made (not snap) about how to work with this customer based on customers fitting his/her profile in the past.

In summary, correctly applied Gladwell's theories about how we process information unconsciously can be used to increase sales, turn products into bestsellers, and alter human behavior. The art of deal making is based on the art of listening and using your experience to bring an idea, service, or product to market. Thus, making the sale has more to do with doing your homework than glibly and blindly going down your memorized sales pitch to any customer who walks through the door.

Helpful Hints:

1. Go into a car showroom and notice where the sales staff are; are they milling around nervously, appear calm and relaxed, appear business-like, and how you are approached by them.
2. Look at how a department store floor area is laid out. Does the flow make sense to the customer—e.g. men's belts by men's wallets.
3. Walk into any service business and notice the customer waiting area. Is it attractive, informative, and friendly?

Peter Drucker: In Remembrance (1909 to 2005)

No other management guru influenced American business more the last fifty years than Peter Drucker. His writings flourished in what we now refer to as the "Information Age," but his HBR articles and books transcended the American corporation and influenced leaders and managers to develop personal skills based on psychological and managerial theories. Of all his traits listed for effective leadership, his foremost tenet was "Listen first, speak last." As a tribute to Drucker the author wishes to offer a few insights into what effective leadership is NOT.

Corporations today are based on an incremental, short-sighted model that promises quarterly financial returns to stockholders at the risk of ethical principles and employee morale. The fact that *Fortune* magazine features the "Best 100 Companies to Work For" each year, attests to the fact that bosses really don't care about their subordinates. Even with 360 evaluations most managers concern themselves with "upstream" news rather than "downstream" news. The fact that the number one complaint of corporate America is one's boss is a fitting testament to the lack of charisma and effective leadership today. The Enron debacle adds to the business lexicon that "Enron gate" is synonymous with poorly defined leadership, mismanagement, and decisions devoid of ethics and sense of fairness. It's not enough to claim ignorance when thousands have lost entire savings because they believed upper management was doing their job.

Most managers today PANIC in lieu of basing sound decisions on basic management principles that Drucker espoused during his illustrious career as consultant and teacher to MBAs and CEOs for five decades. Panic by its very nature implies that decisions are short-sighted, impulsive, arbitrary, and designed to cover up important mistakes, whether intentional or not. If one is unfortunate enough to require ER services due to a critical injury, panic is the last thing one wants to see in the faces of doctors and nurses. Although a life hangs in the balance in the ER, millions of lives are affected by business decisions daily. Trade agreements, tariffs, intellectual property rights, patents, trademarks, confidentiality agreements, ROI (return on investment), to name a few, are reactionary in nature to give a FEW advantage over MANY. Let's take a look at what leads to panic within companies.

No **Planning**: If you don't have a roadmap, then you are relegated to running around in circles looking busy. Drucker said it best in his "HBR Managing for Business Effectiveness" in his 1963 article that "there is surely nothing quite as useless as doing with great efficiency what should not be done at all." How many times have you witnessed companies working a frenetic pace only to achieve few results? I don't know about you but I want my surgeon to draw on my belly with a magic marker before he cuts on me.

No **Assignments**: Work without delegation is chaos. How many times have you seen departments working at cross purposes because of a lack of communication, trust, or knowledge of the bigger picture? The FBI, DEA, CIA, and NSA are notorious for turf battles that limit their effectiveness. If you want a job done right, you have to know the skills of your people and assign jobs accordingly. Project leads with engineering backgrounds generally lack this skill and believe in the axiom that "divide and conquer" is superior to "assess and assign."

No **Notice**: Employees are no different from anyone else and simple reinforcement principles from psychology apply here. While it is true we work for money, recognition is a far superior motivator for maintaining employee performance and morale. Annual company picnics are not the venue to recognize people for a job well done. Parking spaces, employee of the month, gift certificates, time off, public presentations, travel, and educational incentives are important to making folks feel special.

No **Instruction**: There is no substitute for training to eliminate obsolescence and middlescence in the workplace. Unfortunately training is looked at as a waste of time that takes the employee away from production or operations. With long-distance, virtual institutes, staff is not required to leave work to gain knowledge. They can integrate knowledge and theory with case studies from their own venue. Esoteric rhetoric from ivory towers is part of managerial history and there exists much more dynamic interplay between theory and practice.

No **Celebration**: An important coaching tool is to celebrate the successes of your client. American corporations would do well to follow a coaching model when mentoring employees. QA is synonymous with "what's wrong" which leads to less risk taking and entrepreneurial spirit. What is needed in our businesses today are "celebration teams" that not only recognize but inspire and transform our successes that motivate and infuse our workers with energy.

Any of you who have suffered from panic attacks know that this unpleasant experience leads one towards the false belief that one is going to die. Organizations can also develop a "panic" mentality that is based on fear and ignorance. Without planning, assigning, noticing, instructing, and celebrating the successes of your employees, there is no effective leadership, just mediocre management.

Helpful Hints:

1. Read a case study on a company "turnaround" and look for parallels with the "panic" model for successful change.
2. Notice how many consultants operate on a panic model for change and why their effectiveness is diminished after they leave the company.
3. Look at a coaching model for effective leadership and notice how the client is empowered to make a difference.

Final Thoughts

In closing, I wish to offer my comments as a small business owner on what makes for a "good year." Traditionally fiscal years and calendar years are synonymous, although they can differ. The time between Thanksgiving and Christmas is generally "downtime" for most small business owners. Holiday parties, gift cards and exchanges, office decorations, and food fill most offices during December. Our words are kinder and more thoughtful; we are more patient and understanding of one another. We made it through another business cycle with some small profit and good will (also a business term which signifies intangible assets).

But what are we really thankful for? For some owners it might be the downtime needed to recharge our batteries for next year's challenges; for others, it might be a time to recognize those employees who helped us meet our goals and benchmarks. Darrell Royal had a saying when asked about winning the 1970 National Championship game, that "we dance with who brung (sic) us," a reference to his quarterback James Street who started all eleven games that year with a wishbone offense of three talented backs: Ted Coy, Chris Gilbert, and Steve Worster. Charitable donations and gifts limit our net profits to reduce business taxes; we may increase inventories in December to further reduce our "bottom-line" to start out next year fully armed and ready to execute our business plan.

After reading many business bestsellers this past year by former and current CEOs, governmental and non-profit charismatic leaders, I am left with emptiness each December that I couldn't explain but felt in the core of my gut. As small business owners face increasing challenges from globalization and buyouts, we still account for the largest per capita growth in our economy. Small cap stocks are still a good buy in volatile times in large part due to the independence of thought and action that made America great. With cheaper labor supplanting American jobs more corporate types are turning to small business ventures to continue good will towards customers and employees. Witness the boomers who are hitting their sixth decade of life to discover that enthusiasm, intellect, and perseverance do not diminish with age.

Fortune features "Confessions of a CEO," a story about Dominic Orr who rose to the top of the corporate telecom world with two IPOs at the cost of almost losing his family and core values. With the help of a spiritual coach, he re-balanced his life after taking time away from Corporate America to re-center his priorities on family, community, and self. For every Dominic Orr, hundreds of small business owners face the life balance question each day. Many of us work alone or with less than ten employees; we work long hours and wear many hats, only to be reminded that work is not a job, but an opportunity to serve others. We start with a dream that becomes reality with that first sale, first walk-in, or first check. We work from home, office, and laptop to remain competitive in a volatile market of bankruptcies. Most of us will never go public; we will not sit on Boards of Directors; we will pay our fair share of corporate and franchise taxes; we will offer a product or service at a reasonable cost, free of some governmental intervention.

But for those of us who muse each December about why we continue as small business owners, I offer a few of my own thoughts:

- We value the freedom of schedule that permits us to better manage our time.
- We like creating jobs rather than taking them away.
- We are "hands on" managers who see delegation as a sign of weakness.
- We are humbled by our successes and failures.
- We receive satisfaction from effort, not just results.
- We see work as a calling, not just a job.
- We live the American dream of running our own business, devoid of conceit or entitlement.
- We like dealing directly with our customers.

Reflections From a Business Coach

- We are reminded daily of our mistakes and achievements.
- We are privileged to serve others.

Please take time for reflection, enlightenment, and humility. To all small business owners, my hope for you is continued health and success, life balance, and the realization that we are but stewards of financial wealth. For the lucky few, we know the value of this season of *peace and good will*.

Helpful Hints:

1. At this year's office Christmas party notice what is not being said. Typically awards are given to "star" performers while the silent majority look on. What do you really think about when your spouse asks "do we really have to go again?"
2. This December, develop a personal mission statement that balances work, family, community service, and personal growth. Put it into practice in January.
3. Why did you become a small business owner? Were you retreating from the corporate world or putting your own core values into practice?

www.ingramcontent.com/pod-product-compliance
Lightning Source LLC
Chambersburg PA
CBHW071416170526
45165CB00001B/296